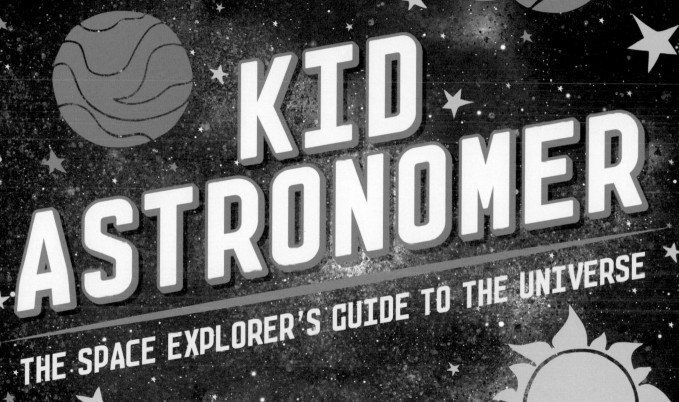

KID ASTRONOMER

THE SPACE EXPLORER'S GUIDE TO THE UNIVERSE

APPLESAUCE PRESS

TABLE OF CONTENTS

*Earth and the Sun,
as seen from space.*

INTRODUCTION

It's hard to imagine what is beyond our planet, but in reality, the universe is much bigger than life on Earth.

Looking up at the sky can tell us a lot about the universe, and ancient astronomers did just that as they started exploring space. During the day, the Sun and clouds show just a hint of what's beyond Earth...but at night, the Moon and stars show us that there is far more out there than first meets the eye.

The invention of the telescope in the early 1600s gave us a new way to look at the sky. Astronomers could see much farther into space—far beyond what merely their eyes could see. They mapped and calculated, and spent years trying to learn more about space.

In the 1960s, we made another huge stride in space exploration by sending humans into outer space! To investigate what lies beyond our world, humans have studied the Moon and stars from spaceships, walked on the Moon, and even lived in outer space in the International Space Station (page 119).

WHAT IS IN SPACE?

Once you leave planet Earth, there is no breathable air in the atmosphere. That's why astronauts have to wear large oxygen tanks when they are outside of their spaceship.

Outer space is black, but that doesn't mean it's empty. Gas, dust, and matter make up most of space, but there are also objects like planets, moons, galaxies, stars, and dwarf planets. There are also smaller objects like meteors, asteroids, and comets that move throughout space.

Two interesting elements of space are supernovas and black holes. When a star runs out of fuel, it explodes; this explosion forms a supernova. Black holes are areas from which nothing—not even light—can escape. These mysteries of space are hard to understand because scientists have not been able to explore them.

Objects in space are not stationary; most travel in an orbit around another object. Sometimes, these moving objects collide.

It's impossible for us to measure the size and age of space. Our explorations have led us to find objects that are billions of years old. Distance in space is measured in light-years, or the distance that light travels in one year.

Despite all of our explorations, we have not yet found evidence of other forms of life in space.

WHY EXPLORE SPACE?

Humans are explorers by nature, and that desire to explore extends far beyond the boundaries of Earth. But our own curiosity is not the only reason to care about what happens in space.

Our lives are ruled by the Sun and Moon; the Sun's rays heat our planet, the Moon's gravity controls the oceans' tides, and together they set our days and nights. Also important is the fact that other objects in space are not stationary and are constantly moving around our planet; understanding the objects in the universe and their location helps us to better understand our own planet.

Although we have not yet found evidence of life on other planets, scientists hope to determine if there are other planets that could support life. This doesn't just mean looking for aliens. It means that scientists are looking for planets with appropriate temperatures, a stable atmosphere, and sufficient water; together, these three things would allow plants or people to grow and thrive. As of now, we don't know of any other planets that humans could live on, but scientists are always looking for planets where this might be possible.

Space is made up of matter and elements, many of which are also present on Earth. Because of our own ever-changing climate, it is important for us to understand the different matter and forces in the universe that could have the potential to give us new forms of energy.

Our Sun (center) and its solar system, from left to right: Pluto (a dwarf planet), Neptune, Uranus, Saturn, Jupiter, Mars, Earth, Venus, and Mercury.

OUR SOLAR SYSTEM

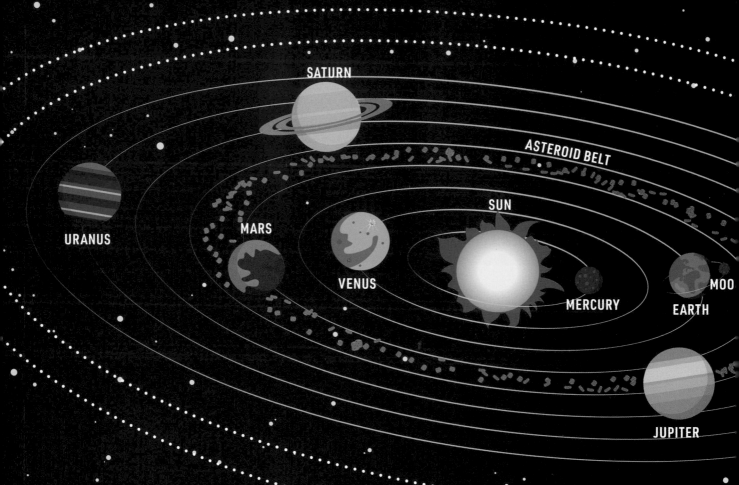

SATURN

ASTEROID BELT

URANUS

MARS

VENUS

SUN

MERCURY

MOO

EARTH

JUPITER

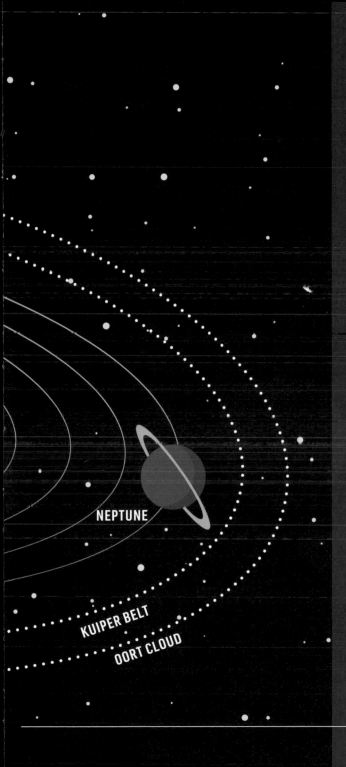

NEPTUNE

KUIPER BELT

OORT CLOUD

CORNER OF THE UNIVERSE

Welcome to our solar system! Our solar system is one of countless solar systems in the Milky Way, our home galaxy. Each solar system has at least one star at its center—ours is the Sun! Everything in our solar system is held together by the Sun's gravity.

The eight known planets in our solar system—including our home planet, Earth—all move around the Sun in what's called an orbit. The circles on this map represent the planets' different orbits; notice that some planets are much closer to the Sun, but they all move around it.

Other than the Sun, the planets are the biggest things in our solar system. But it's home to lots of other interesting things, too! There are the moons around many of the planets. There are asteroids, comets, and meteors that fly through space, including the ones in the enormous asteroid belt between Jupiter and Mars. There are dwarf planets, too, plus lots of mysterious dark matter and dark energy that scientists don't fully understand yet.

Way out past Neptune is the distant, icy region known as the Kuiper belt. And even farther than that, there's the Oort cloud, which scientists think goes around the whole solar system like a bubble. And who knows? There might even be other living things somewhere in our solar system!

PLANETS
IN OUR AMAZING SOLAR SYSTEM

JUPITER

Jupiter is by far the biggest planet in our solar system. Jupiter is a gas giant, and the Great Red Spot on its surface is actually an enormous storm made of gaseous clouds.

NEPTUNE

Windy, icy, and enormous, Neptune is farther away from Earth than any other planet in our solar system. Neptune's gaseous atmosphere makes it look blue, but it's so far away that it can't be seen from Earth by the naked eye.

URANUS

Uranus is a massive ice giant. It has 13 rings, and it's the only planet in our entire solar system that spins on its side instead of upright.

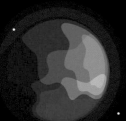

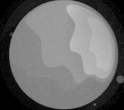

SATURN

Gas giant Saturn is the second-largest planet in our solar system. It's famous for its beautiful rings, which are made up of pieces of rock and ice.

MARS

Often called the Red Planet, Mars is cold, rocky, and about half the size of Earth. It's been visited by many spacecraft from Earth, including rovers that have explored its surface.

VENUS

Venus is closer to Earth than any other planet. It is the hottest planet in our solar system, and while most planets spin from west to east, Venus rotates the opposite way.

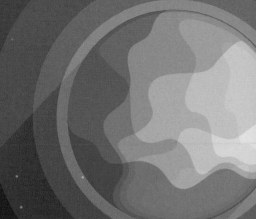

MERCURY

The smallest planet in our solar system, Mercury is also the closest to the Sun. Mercury spins slowly, but it moves through its orbit around the Sun faster than any other planet.

EARTH

Our home! Unlike any other planet in our solar system, Earth has liquid water on its surface, which makes it a great place for life to thrive.

WHAT IS A PLANET?

According to the International Astronomical Union, in order for an object in space to be considered a planet, it must orbit a sun, but it cannot be the moon of another space object. A planet must also be round and large enough to move objects (such as asteroids and comets) out of its way to continue its orbit. Because of the last requirement, Pluto—formerly considered a planet—was recategorized as a dwarf planet in 2006.

Our solar system has eight objects that are officially classified as planets, and are typically ordered by how far away they are from the Sun: Mercury, Venus, Earth, Mars, Jupiter, Saturn, Uranus, and Neptune.

THE TYPES OF PLANETS

There are three different types of planets in our solar system: terrestrial, gas giant, and ice giant. The first four planets from the Sun—Mercury, Venus, Earth, and Mars—are terrestrial planets. This type of planet has a rocky, solid surface. The next two planets—Jupiter and Saturn—are gas giant planets. The opposite of terrestrial planets, the gas giant planets are mostly made up of gas. The last two planets—Uranus and Neptune—are ice giant planets because they are primarily made up of ice.

All the planets in our solar system move around the Sun in an orbit. An orbit is the path that one object in space takes around another object. Most of the planets have orbits that are almost circles, but orbits come in different shapes. For instance, Mercury's orbit is egg shaped! The time it takes for a planet to complete one orbit is the length of a year for that planet. So you might have guessed—correctly—that Earth's orbit around the Sun takes 365 days.

Another thing that's different for different planets is their rotation. All planets turn on an imaginary line called on axis, which runs through the middle of the planet like the core of an apple. When a planet spins around once on its axis, that's one rotation. The time it takes for a planet to complete one rotation is the length of a day on that planet—for us on Earth, one rotation takes 24 hours.

TERRESTRIAL

GAS GIANTS

ICE GIANTS

PLANETS IN OUR SOLAR SYSTEM

AND BEYOND

The word "planet" comes from the Greek word "planetes," meaning "wanderer." Until the 1990s, we only knew about the planets in our solar system. But now, we have discovered many planets that orbit other stars. These are called extrasolar planets or exoplanets. Scientists estimate that there are at least 100 billion planets in our galaxy!

Closer to home, some scientists have begun to question if there is a ninth planet lurking far behind Neptune. If it existed, it would help explain the movement of some objects in the Kuiper belt (page 98). But that movement could also be the result of a grapefruit-sized black hole or the collective influence of several small objects, so no one is really sure yet.

PLANETARY PARTICULARS

Some planets have rings around them; others don't.
Some planets have moons that orbit them; others
don't. Some planets are enormous, while others are
small—Jupiter is almost 30 times as wide as Mercury!
The incredible variety among the planets is part of
what makes our solar system such a fascinating place.

MERCURY

SPACE SPEEDER

Mercury is named after a famously fast god from Roman mythology. That's because it's the speediest of the planets—following an egg-shaped orbit, it makes a full trip around the Sun in only 88 Earth days. Many of the craters on Mercury's rocky surface are named after writers, artists, and musicians. There's even a colorful crater named for Dr. Seuss!

SIZE (radius): 1,516 miles (2,439.7 km)

MOONS: 0

DISTANCE FROM SUN: 36 million miles (58 million km)

TIME TO ORBIT SUN (one year): 88 Earth days

COSMIC DATA: Like Venus, Earth, and Mars, Mercury is a terrestrial planet. Its rocky surface has lots of craters and looks similar to the surface of Earth's moon. Mercury is an incredibly hot planet during the day and extremely cold at night; daytime temperatures can reach 800°F (430°C), and at night, the temperature can drop to -290°F (-180°C). One day on Mercury (the time it takes for the planet to rotate once) takes about 59 Earth days.

VENUS

A WILD WORLD

Things are never dull on Venus! It features enormous volcanoes and tall mountains, and acidic clouds blow across its surface, powered by winds as strong as hurricanes. Some scientists even think that there may once have been water on Venus's surface. Venus is named for the Roman goddess of beauty and love.

CAN YOU TAKE THE HEAT?

Venus is the hottest planet in our solar system, even though Mercury is closer to the Sun. That's because Venus has a dense atmosphere made up mostly of carbon dioxide, and all that thick gas keeps heat trapped close to the planet. The temperature on Venus is higher than 800°F (430°C)!

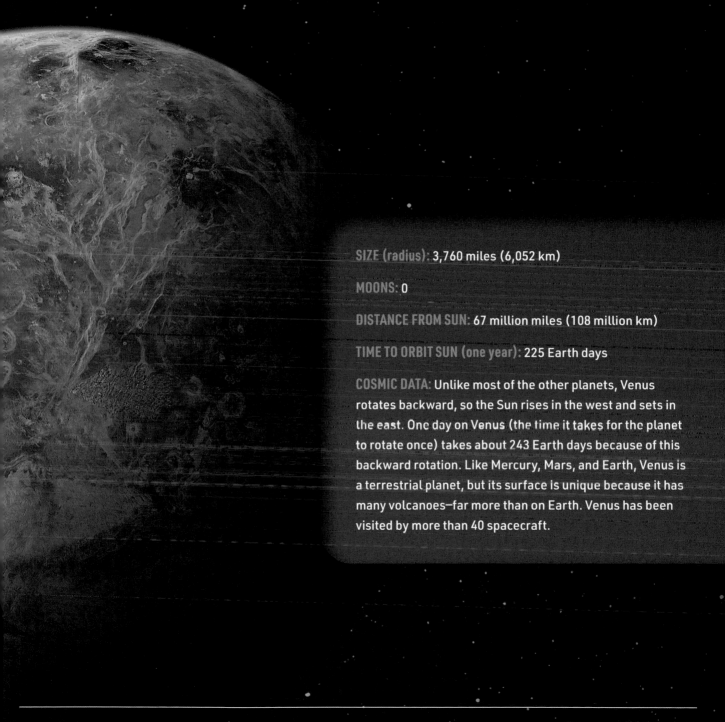

SIZE (radius): 3,760 miles (6,052 km)

MOONS: 0

DISTANCE FROM SUN: 67 million miles (108 million km)

TIME TO ORBIT SUN (one year): 225 Earth days

COSMIC DATA: Unlike most of the other planets, Venus rotates backward, so the Sun rises in the west and sets in the east. One day on Venus (the time it takes for the planet to rotate once) takes about 243 Earth days because of this backward rotation. Like Mercury, Mars, and Earth, Venus is a terrestrial planet, but its surface is unique because it has many volcanoes—far more than on Earth. Venus has been visited by more than 40 spacecraft.

EARTH

OUR OWN HOME

Earth isn't just humans' home. It's also the home of all the living things in our solar system—as far as we know, anyway! One of the reasons that Earth is unique is that its air is perfect for creatures like us to breathe—78% nitrogen, 21% oxygen, plus very small amounts of other gases. About 4.5 billion years ago, Earth formed out of clouds of dust and gas that were pulled together by gravity. The other planets are named after ancient Roman or Greek gods, but not Earth—its name comes from English and German words that just mean "the ground."

SEASONS IN SPACE

On Earth, the seasons each year happen because of our planet's tilted axis. Because Earth spins at an angle, the Northern Hemisphere is tilted toward the Sun during one part of the year, while the Southern Hemisphere is tilted toward the Sun during a different part of the year. This unequal heat from the Sun is what gives us summer, fall, winter, and spring.

WATER WORLD

Earth has a rocky surface, but it's also considered an ocean planet. That's because water covers about 70% of Earth's surface!

SIZE (radius): 3,959 miles (6,371 km)

MOONS: 1

DISTANCE FROM THE SUN: 93 million miles (150 million km)

TIME TO ORBIT SUN (one year): 365 days

COSMIC DATA: Like Mercury, Venus, and Mars, Earth is a terrestrial planet. While the surface of our home planet has canyons, plains, and mountains, it is mostly covered in water. Earth is the only life-supporting planet within our solar system; the atmosphere here is mostly nitrogen and oxygen, allowing us to breathe and protecting Earth from any incoming meteors or asteroids. Earth is also the only planet in our solar system with one moon. Astronauts have spent a long time studying our Moon and viewing Earth from space.

MARS

THE RED PLANET

Mars is a chilly desert planet covered in rocks, canyons, and dead volcanoes. It's named after the ancient Roman god of war, because the planet's red surface looks like it could be covered in blood. But really, Mars looks red to us because its soil contains a lot of iron, which turns red when it touches the oxygen in Mars's atmosphere. In other words, Mars is just rusty!

Mars has a lot of interesting landmarks on its surface, but one of the most exciting is a volcano called Olympus Mons. Olympus Mons is three times taller than Mt. Everest! And if its base were on Earth, it would be big enough to cover the entire state of New Mexico. Even though it probably hasn't erupted in millions of years, Olympus Mons is the largest volcano in the entire solar system.

RED ROVERS

Scientists believe that billions of years ago, Mars may have been a very different place. Long ago, Mars could have had a warmer climate and liquid water—perhaps even living creatures! Scientists know all this thanks to the many spacecraft that have explored Mars over the years. Some of them orbit Mars to study it from afar, while some spacecraft—called rovers—land on the surface of the planet itself. Other than Earth, Mars is the planet that humans have been able to study the most. That's because it's relatively close to Earth and has a rocky surface that spacecraft can land on.

Olympus Mons

SIZE (radius): 2,106 miles (3,390 km)

MOONS: 2

DISTANCE FROM SUN: 142 million miles (228 million km)

TIME TO ORBIT SUN (one year): 687 Earth days

COSMIC DATA: Like Mercury, Venus, and Earth, Mars is a terrestrial planet with a very rocky surface. Mars has been nicknamed the Red Planet, because the minerals that make up its surface have a distinctive rusty color. Mars has two moons, Phobos (page 46) and Deimos (page 47). Mars has a similar day length to Earth, with one rotation taking about 24 hours, but—because it is farther away from the Sun—a year on Mars is almost double the length of a year on Earth. Currently, scientists have found no evidence of life on Mars, but there are ongoing space missions to help us decide whether the planet could support life.

JUPITER

KING OF THE PLANETS

Jupiter is the biggest planet in our solar system—by a lot! Jupiter is more than twice as massive as all of the other planets in our solar system put together. Or, think of it this way: measured across its equator, Jupiter is as wide as 11 Earths put together. But even though it's huge, Jupiter isn't solid. It's a gas giant, which means that instead of a solid surface like Earth's or Mars's, it has a swirling, misty surface made of gas and liquid. Jupiter also has over 75 moons, and it is named after the ancient Roman god who was known as the king of all the other gods.

Days on Jupiter are quick: it only takes about 10 Earth hours for Jupiter to make one full rotation. But on the other hand, it takes Jupiter a long time to orbit the Sun, which means that years on Jupiter are much longer than years on Earth. One Jupiter year is equal to about 12 Earth years!

THE GREAT RED SPOT

Jupiter is famous for its Great Red Spot. It may look like the spot is always the same, but in fact, it's changing all the time—because it's actually an enormous storm! The Great Red Spot is bigger than the entire Earth, and the storm has been going on for hundreds of years. Like other storms on Jupiter (and the rest of the planet's surface), it's made out of windswept clouds.

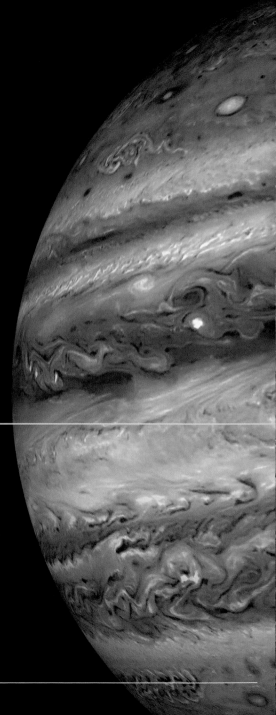

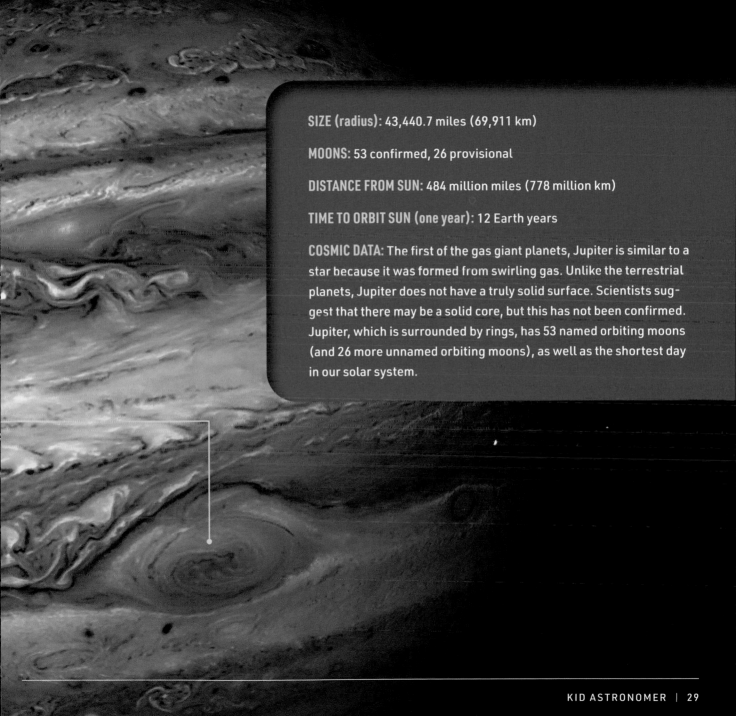

SIZE (radius): 43,440.7 miles (69,911 km)

MOONS: 53 confirmed, 26 provisional

DISTANCE FROM SUN: 484 million miles (778 million km)

TIME TO ORBIT SUN (one year): 12 Earth years

COSMIC DATA: The first of the gas giant planets, Jupiter is similar to a star because it was formed from swirling gas. Unlike the terrestrial planets, Jupiter does not have a truly solid surface. Scientists suggest that there may be a solid core, but this has not been confirmed. Jupiter, which is surrounded by rings, has 53 named orbiting moons (and 26 more unnamed orbiting moons), as well as the shortest day in our solar system.

A GLORIOUS GIANT

Like Jupiter, Saturn is a gas giant—it doesn't have a solid surface, and it's mostly made of hydrogen and helium. Saturn is also huge! It's the second-biggest planet in our solar system. If you lined up nine Earths next to each other, they would be almost as wide as Saturn—and that's not including its famous rings.

Of all the fascinating things about Saturn, its incredible rings are its true claim to fame. It has seven beautiful rings, and they reach as far as 175,000 miles (280,000 km) away from Saturn itself. The rings sometimes look solid, but they're made of billions of bits of floating rock and ice. Scientists think that these bits used to be pieces of comets, asteroids, and other space rocks before they got pulled apart by Saturn's gravity. Some of the pieces of ice and rock in Saturn's rings are as tiny as grains of sand (or even tinier!), but some of them are much, much bigger. Some pieces are as big as a car or a house—and a couple are the size of mountains!

MANY MOONS

Saturn is famous for its moons too. There are over 50 that have already been discovered, plus over 20 more that scientists are still working on confirming. Saturn's name comes from the ancient Roman god of farming and wealth.

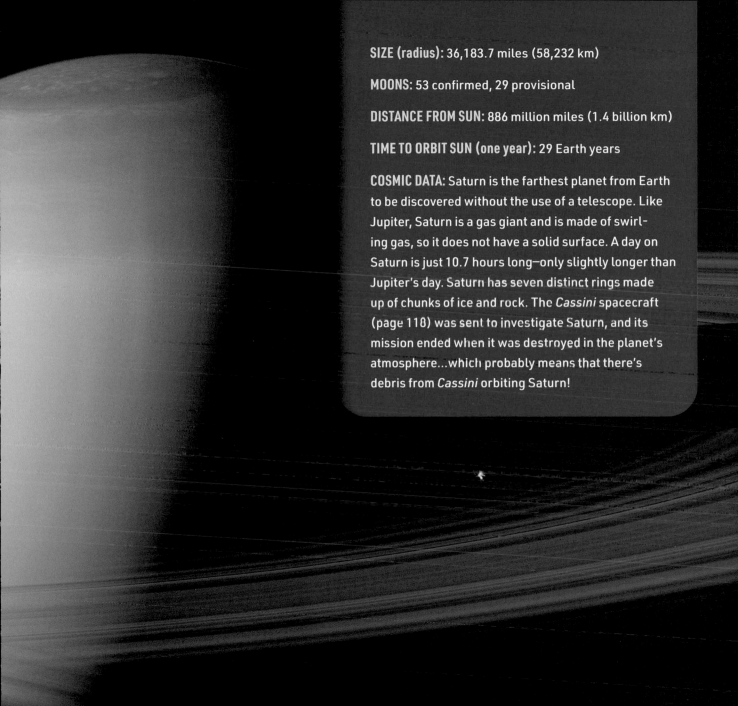

SIZE (radius): 36,183.7 miles (58,232 km)

MOONS: 53 confirmed, 29 provisional

DISTANCE FROM SUN: 886 million miles (1.4 billion km)

TIME TO ORBIT SUN (one year): 29 Earth years

COSMIC DATA: Saturn is the farthest planet from Earth to be discovered without the use of a telescope. Like Jupiter, Saturn is a gas giant and is made of swirling gas, so it does not have a solid surface. A day on Saturn is just 10.7 hours long—only slightly longer than Jupiter's day. Saturn has seven distinct rings made up of chunks of ice and rock. The *Cassini* spacecraft (page 118) was sent to investigate Saturn, and its mission ended when it was destroyed in the planet's atmosphere...which probably means that there's debris from *Cassini* orbiting Saturn!

SIZE (radius): 15,759.2 miles (25,362 km)

MOONS: 27

DISTANCE FROM SUN: 1.8 billion miles (2.9 billion km)

TIME TO ORBIT SUN (one year): 84 Earth years

COSMIC DATA: Uranus is the first of the ice giants, and most of the planet is made up of icy material around a solid core. Uranus was the first planet discovered through the use of a telescope, and only one spacecraft (*Voyager 2*, page 112) has ever flown by the planet. Uranus has 13 rings around it, as well as 27 moons—and each moon is named after a character created by the writers William Shakespeare and Alexander Pope. Uranus itself is named after the Greek god of the sky.

URANUS

SIDE SPINNER

The most unusual thing about Uranus is its rotation. Like Venus, it rotates from east to west—the opposite direction from most of the planets! Plus, Uranus is the only planet that spins on its side. That gives Uranus very extreme seasons, because the Sun shines directly on one end of the planet for so long. When that happens, it's winter on the other half of the planet—for 21 Earth years straight!

ICE GIANTS

Both Uranus and Neptune are known as ice giants, which means that their surfaces are made of a foggy mixture of methane, ammonia, and water. The methane is what makes both planets look blue! Underneath, Uranus and Neptune each have a smaller core made of rock. Since they're so cold and far away from Earth, neither planet has ever been studied up close by humans. *Voyager 2* flew by Uranus and Neptune on its way out of our solar system, but no other spacecraft has visited them.

NEPTUNE

WINDY WORLD

Neptune is farther away from the Sun than any other planet in our solar system. It's only a little smaller than Uranus, but unlike all the other planets, it's so far away that it can't even be seen with the human eye alone—we have to use telescopes to look at it. Neptune is cold, dark, and extremely windy! It's covered in clouds made of frozen methane, which blow around in winds about five times as strong as the strongest winds on Earth. The winds on Neptune move almost as fast as a fighter jet! Neptune also has a few faint rings that are difficult to see.

RULER OF THE OCEAN

Neptune has 14 moons, and all of them are named after sea deities and water nymphs from Greek myths. That's appropriate, because Neptune itself is named after the Roman god of the ocean. Neptune is in good company too—in mythology, his brothers are Jupiter and Pluto!

SIZE (radius): 15,299.4 miles (24,622 km)

MOONS: 14

DISTANCE FROM SUN: 2.8 billion miles (4.5 billion km)

TIME TO ORBIT SUN (one year): 165 Earth years

COSMIC DATA: Neptune, the other ice giant, is the farthest planet from the Sun in our solar system, and, like Uranus, is made up of icy material surrounding a small core. Neptune is known for being the windiest planet in the solar system. It has five known rings and 14 moons. The dwarf planet Pluto is usually farther away from the Sun than Neptune, but Pluto has a strange orbit path that sometimes brings it closer to the Sun than Neptune.

OUR MOON

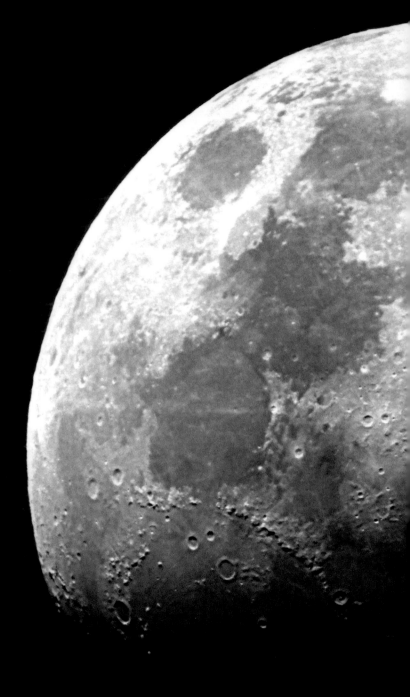

Look up into the sky at night, and you can usually see Earth's moon. A lot of the planets have several moons around them, and some have many. Astronomers started discovering moons in the 1600s and were surprised to learn that planets other than Earth had them. Moons are objects in space that naturally orbit around a particular planet. Even dwarf planets can have moons. A variety of different things can be found on a moon's surface—ice, mountains, craters, and even volcanoes! Even though scientists estimate that there are at least 181 moons in our solar system, humans have only set foot on one: Earth's moon.

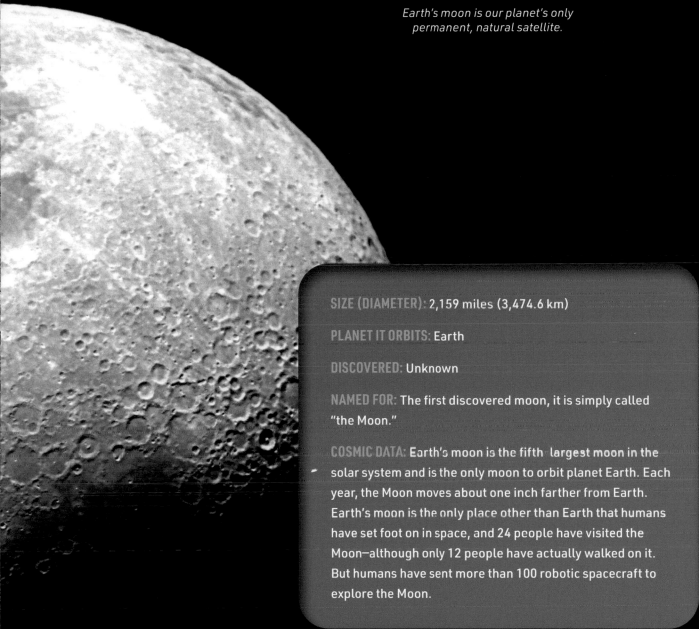

Earth's moon is our planet's only permanent, natural satellite.

SIZE (DIAMETER): 2,159 miles (3,474.6 km)

PLANET IT ORBITS: Earth

DISCOVERED: Unknown

NAMED FOR: The first discovered moon, it is simply called "the Moon."

COSMIC DATA: Earth's moon is the fifth-largest moon in the solar system and is the only moon to orbit planet Earth. Each year, the Moon moves about one inch farther from Earth. Earth's moon is the only place other than Earth that humans have set foot on in space, and 24 people have visited the Moon—although only 12 people have actually walked on it. But humans have sent more than 100 robotic spacecraft to explore the Moon.

THE MOON'S SURFACE

Earth's moon is a terrestrial body, meaning it's made up of rock, dirt, and dust, like Earth is. Long ago, the surface of the Moon was dotted with active volcanoes—much like Earth—but they have been dormant for millions of years. Gravity on the surface of the Moon is only one-sixth of the gravity on Earth, meaning that if you weighed 100 lbs. on Earth, you would only be about 17 lbs. on the Moon!

If you set a green pea next to a US nickel, you'd get a sense of how big the Moon is compared to Earth.

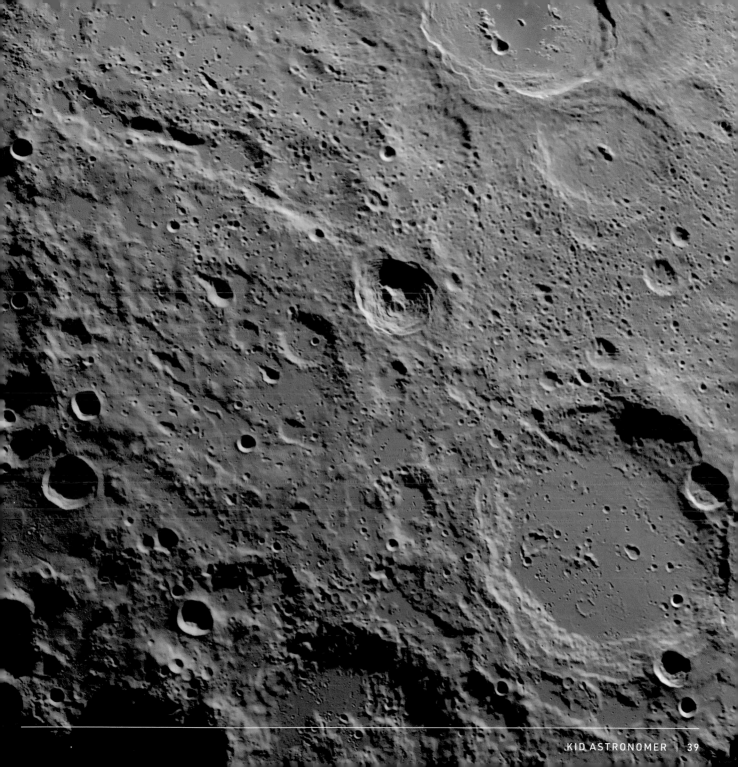

LUNAR ATMOSPHERE AND CLIMATE

Since the Moon's atmosphere is nearly nonexistent compared to Earth's atmosphere, the Moon is not as well defended against meteors and asteroids. That is why the Moon's surface is made up of craters, boulders, and powder. Because the Moon has almost no atmosphere, it also has no weather, meaning that its surface is a preserved record of its history. This also means that the temperature on the Moon is entirely up to the sun. When in full Sun, the surface of the Moon can reach 260°F (126°C), and the temperature falls to -280°F (-173°C) in full darkness.

Fun Fact: Because the surface of the Moon has no wind or any other form of weather, the footprints left behind by the astronauts are still on the surface of the Moon today and will be for millions of years—unless they're hit by an asteroid, of course!

OUR NEAREST NEIGHBOR

Scientists think that the Moon was formed billions of years ago when an object the size of Mars smashed into Earth. Now, our Moon orbits Earth, and it's the only other place in the solar system that human beings have visited in person. There are over 150 moons in our solar system, but until Galileo discovered four of Jupiter's moons in 1610, no one knew about any of them. That's why ours is just called "the Moon."

CLIMATE CONTROL

The Moon plays a huge role in shaping the climate on Earth. Because of the Moon's gravitational pull, Earth is more stable on its axis, which means that things like temperature and weather stay more stable too—and humans have an easier time living here! The Moon's gravity is also what causes the oceans' steady tides.

OTHER MOONS

MARS'S MOONS

WARRIOR MOONS

Mars has two moons, **Phobos** and **Deimos**. They're named after the mythological sons of Ares, the Greek god of war (the Greek version of the Roman god Mars). Phobos and Deimos are both quite small compared to many of the other moons in our solar system. They're both made of a mixture of rock and ice, which scientists think might mean that they were once asteroids that got caught in Mars's gravity.

PHOBOS

Phobos is bigger than Deimos. It is most notable for the enormous crater on its surface, which is called Stickney. Stickney is six miles wide! Phobos also has long grooves across its surface, like giant scratch marks. Phobos's orbit around Mars is a spiral, which means that it is always moving a tiny bit closer to Mars. So within about 50 million years, it could crash into Mars. Or, it might break into pieces and become a ring around Mars.

SIZE (diameter): 13.8 miles (22.2 km)

PLANET IT ORBITS: Mars

DISCOVERED: 1877

NAMED FOR: Son of Ares in Greek mythology

COSMIC DATA: Discovered by Asaph Hall, Phobos is mostly made of rock. This moon is slowly moving closer to Mars—about 6 feet (1.8 m) every 100 years.

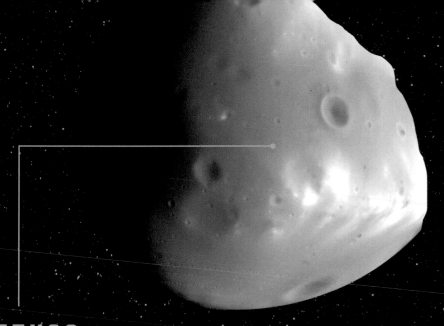

DEIMOS

Deimos is the smaller of Mars's two moons. Deimos has a lumpy surface with some craters, but it doesn't have any giant craters or grooves like Phobos. Someday, scientists might try to use Deimos or Phobos as bases to examine Mars from. That's because the moons are close enough to the planet that they could launch rovers between them.

NEVER GIVE UP

Both Phobos and Deimos were discovered in 1877. The astronomer who was searching for them almost quit trying, but his wife encouraged him to keep going, and he discovered Deimos the next night!

JUPITER'S MOONS

GIANTS, VOLCANOES, AND HIDDEN OCEANS

Jupiter has at least 79 moons! So far, scientists have named 53 of them. The four largest of Jupiter's moons were discovered a long time ago, in 1610. In fact, they were the first moons ever discovered beyond Earth's moon. Because Italian astronomer Galileo Galilei discovered them, these four moons are called the Galilean satellites: **Io**, **Europa**, **Ganymede**, and **Callisto**.

IO

Io is covered in volcanoes. Because Jupiter's gravity is so strong, it pulls on the surface of Io, creating waves made of solid ground! The eruptions on Io can reach several miles upward, and they can even be seen from Earth using powerful telescopes.

SIZE (diameter): 2,264 miles (3,643.2 km)

PLANET IT ORBITS: Jupiter

DISCOVERED: 1610

NAMED FOR: A woman in Greek mythology

COSMIC DATA: Of all the objects in our solar system, Io has the most volcanic activity; there are estimated to be hundreds of volcanoes on this moon. Io's orbit takes it through Jupiter's magnetic force, which gives this moon its own electrical charge. Like Europa (page 50), Ganymede (page 52), and Callisto (page 53), Io was discovered by Galileo.

Some of Io's volcanic eruptions send lava plumes dozens of miles into space.

EUROPA

Europa has an icy surface at least 10 miles thick, which most likely covers an enormous ocean made of salt water. If scientists are right about Europa's hidden ocean, it holds twice as much water as all of Earth's oceans combined! Because of all that water, Europa is one of the most likely places in the solar system for discovering life as we know it.

SIZE (diameter): 1,939.7 miles (3,121.6 km)

PLANET IT ORBITS: Jupiter

DISCOVERED: 1610

NAMED FOR: A woman in Greek mythology (the continent Europe was also named for her)

COSMIC DATA: Europa is an icy moon with lines across its surface caused by breaks in the ice; these breaks are filled with a reddish-brown material. Scientists have been very interested in this material, and in the next few years, hope to directly study it with a new spacecraft called the *Europa Clipper*. It will take several years to get to its destination, but once the Clipper—equipped with cameras and radar—has reached Jupiter and begins orbiting, it will be able to study Europa with each "flyby."

Approximately the size of Earth's moon, Europa has shown evidence of potentially having everything needed to support life; proving this will be the most critical element of the Europa Clipper's mission.

GANYMEDE

Ganymede is the biggest moon in our whole solar system. It's even larger than Mercury! Ganymede is also the only moon that has its own magnetic field, which creates streams of glowing gas over its icy surface.

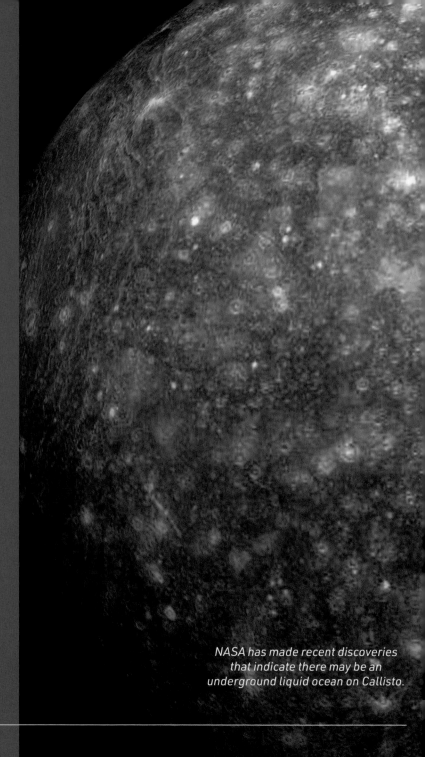

NASA has made recent discoveries that indicate there may be an underground liquid ocean on Callisto.

CALLISTO

Callisto has more craters than anything else in our solar system. Its craters are mostly very old, but some newer activity on Callisto's icy surface makes scientists think that there could be an ocean of salt water underneath. That means that, like Europa, it's possible that Callisto could support life!

SIZE (diameter): 2,985 miles (4,800 km)

PLANET IT ORBITS: Jupiter

DISCOVERED: 1610

NAMED FOR: A nymph in Greek mythology

COSMIC DATA: Callisto is the third-largest moon in our solar system—almost as large as the planet Mercury. Callisto was originally discovered by Galileo and was the first moon found to be orbiting a planet other than Earth. Callisto is one of the oldest objects in the solar system and is estimated to be about 4 million years old.

SATURN'S MOONS

MOONS EVERY WHICH WAY

Saturn has 82 moons, and 53 of them are officially confirmed so far. There is a ton of variety among Saturn's moons—they take lots of different shapes (for example, Hyperion looks like a sponge!), and they range from being as small as a football stadium to larger than Mercury.

ENCELADUS

Among the most interesting of Saturn's moons is **Enceladus,** which hides an ocean of water under its icy surface and also seems to have all the elements necessary to form life as we know it.

SIZE (diameter): 313 miles (504 km)

PLANET IT ORBITS: Saturn

DISCOVERED: 1789

NAMED FOR: A giant in Greek mythology

COSMIC DATA: Enceladus is an icy moon that was discovered by William Herschel; the temperature on this moon is extremely cold at about -330°F (-201°C). There is an ocean beneath its surface, and continuous eruptions spray liquid into space through cracks in the icy crust. Enceladus is Saturn's sixth-largest moon, but it is still fairly small. For comparison, the planet is about as wide across as the US state of Arizona. This moon's smooth, icy surface makes it the most reflective body in our solar system.

The ocean spray from Enceladus reaches so far out into space that it can be sampled by spacecraft.

RHEA

Rhea is Saturn's second-largest moon, but it's nowhere near as big as Titan. Its surface features lots of canyons and craters, and it also has at least one ring around it! Rhea has a very thin atmosphere (infused with oxygen and carbon dioxide) called an exosphere, which the *Cassini* spacecraft detected in 2010. It was the first time a spacecraft directly captured molecules of an oxygen atmosphere at a world other than Earth!

SIZE (diameter): 949.2 miles (1,527.6 km)

PLANET IT ORBITS: Saturn

DISCOVERED: 1672

NAMED FOR: A goddess in Greek mythology

COSMIC DATA: The spacecraft *Cassini*, named after the astronomer who discovered this moon, found evidence of a ring; this was the first time that a ring had been discovered around a moon. Scientists theorize that Rhea—the second largest of Saturn's moons—is made up of three-quarters ice and one-quarter rock.

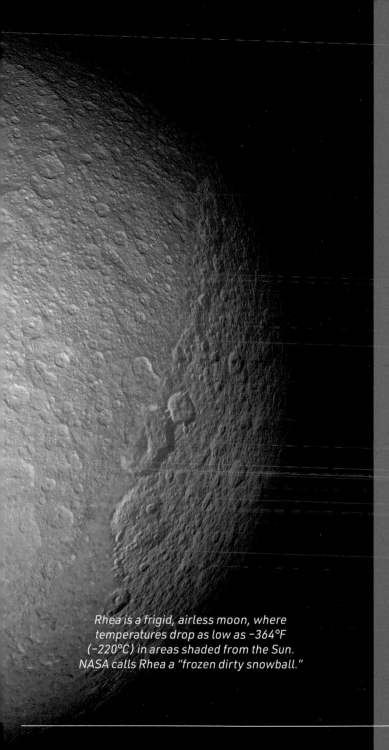

Rhea is a frigid, airless moon, where temperatures drop as low as −364°F (−220°C) in areas shaded from the Sun. NASA calls Rhea a "frozen dirty snowball."

TITAN

Saturn's biggest moon, Titan, is the only place in our solar system besides Earth that's known to have liquid flowing on its surface. But on Titan, the rivers and lakes aren't made of water—they're made of liquid compounds like methane and ethane! Titan's surface is made of water ice, and it might have a water ocean hiding underneath.

IAPETUS

Iapetus, Saturn's third-largest moon, is unusual
because its two hemispheres reflect light very
differently: one is extremely dark, and the other
is much brighter. Scientists aren't certain why
that is, but it might have to do with Iapetus's very
slow rotation. Some parts face the Sun for long
enough that the different hemispheres might
have wildly different temperatures. It might also
be that the dark part of Iapetus is covered with
dust that flies off another moon, Phoebe.

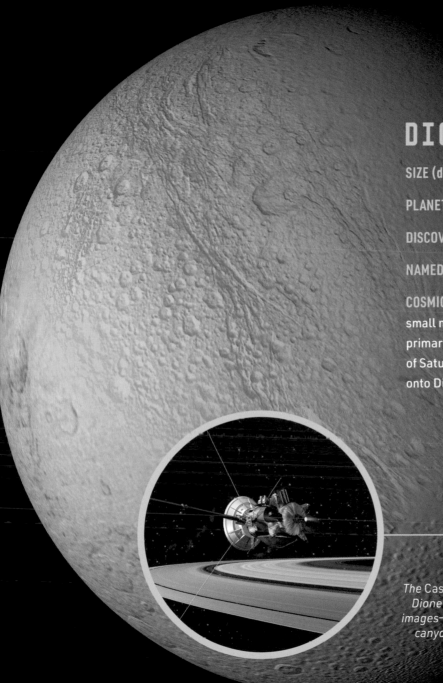

DIONE

SIZE (diameter): 697.7 miles (1,122.8 km)

PLANET IT ORBITS: Saturn

DISCOVERED: 1684

NAMED FOR: A goddess in Greek mythology

COSMIC DATA: Giovanni Cassini discovered this small moon. Scientists suspect that Dione is primarily made up of a dense core and ice. One of Saturn's rings sends ice powder (like smoke) onto Dione.

The Cassini *spacecraft spent years studying Dione and provided scientists with many images—including views of the long, winding canyons that cross this moon's surface.*

MIRANDA

UMBRIEL

TITANIA

ARIEL

URANUS'S MOONS

SHAKESPEAREAN SATELLITES

Uranus's moons have an unusual distinction: they're the most well-read moons! That's because most of them are named after characters from William Shakespeare's plays. Five of Uranus's moons are bigger than the rest, and there's also a group of eight smaller moons that are so close together that scientists don't know why they don't crash into each other. Uranus has 27 moons altogether, and they make up a unique cast of characters.

MIRANDA, UMBRIEL, TITANIA, ARIEL

There's **Miranda**, which features giant canyons that go 12 times as deep as Earth's Grand Canyon. There's **Umbriel**, which is ancient and very dark—except for a mysterious bright spot on one side. There's **Titania**, which is Uranus's largest moon and was named for the queen of the fairies in *A Midsummer Night's Dream*. And don't forget **Ariel**, the brightest of Uranus's moons and probably the youngest.

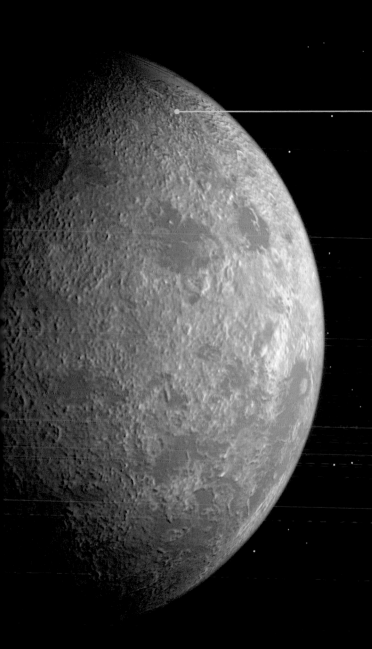

OBERON

Oberon may be the oldest moon orbiting Uranus. It has the most craters of all Uranus's moons, which indicates that it has been hit by many foreign space objects. The nine most distinct craters are named for male Shakespearean characters, from Hamlet to Romeo to Macbeth.

SIZE (diameter): 946.2 miles (1,522.8 km)

PLANET IT ORBITS: Uranus

DISCOVERED: 1787

NAMED FOR: King of the fairies in Shakespeare's *A Midsummer Night's Dream*

COSMIC DATA: Discovered by William Herschel, Oberon is Uranus's second-largest moon. Oberon is made up of equal parts ice and rock; its surface has lots of craters and at least one mountain.

NEPTUNE'S MOONS

DARK AND MYSTERIOUS

Neptune has 14 moons in all, and they're an odd bunch. Many of them are dark compared to most other objects in our solar system, and because they're so far away, they're more mysterious to us than moons closer to Earth. **Triton** is the largest, and it has ice volcanoes that shoot liquid chemicals into the air—the chemicals immediately freeze and become snow! There's also **Proteus**, which has an odd, lumpy shape, and **Nereid**, which has the most irregular orbit of any moon, as far as scientists know. In fact, several of Neptune's moons have unusual orbits.

Despite being one of the coldest, Triton is also one of the four bodies—including Earth—that are volcanically active in our solar system. Neptune can be seen to the right of this image.

TRITON

Triton is the only large moon in our solar system that has an orbit in the opposite direction of its planet's rotation. That's called a retrograde orbit.

SIZE (diameter): 1,680 miles (2,700 km)

PLANET IT ORBITS: Neptune

DISCOVERED: 1846

NAMED FOR: Son of Poseidon in Greek mythology

COSMIC DATA: Triton is the largest of Neptune's moons and was discovered by William Lassell just 17 days after the planet Neptune was discovered. Triton is one of the coldest objects in our solar system, with temperatures of −391°F (−235°C) and an icy surface that reflects sunlight.

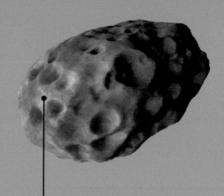

NEREID

Nereid orbits very far from Neptune. It takes almost a full Earth year for Nereid to complete one orbit! Many moons have circular orbits, but not Nereid—it's much farther from Neptune at one end of its orbit than at the other end.

NESO AND PSAMATHE

Neso and Psamathe are tiny moons with similar orbits. Their orbits take them farther away from their planet than almost any other moons in our solar system. They orbit so far from Neptune that it takes them 26 Earth years to complete one orbit!

PLUTO'S MOONS

FABULOUS FIVE

Pluto—which is now classified as a dwarf planet—has just five moons. Scientists think that all five were formed at the same time, when Pluto smashed into some other object in the Kuiper belt (page 98) very early in the history of the solar system. Four of Pluto's moons are quite small. **Nix** and **Hydra** were both discovered in 2005 by scientists using the Hubble Space Telescope (page 114). **Kerberos** and **Styx** are both tiny (possibly fewer than 10 miles across!), and they were discovered even more recently: Kerberos was discovered in 2011, and Styx was discovered in 2012.

But **Charon** is much bigger—it's almost half the size of Pluto itself! That makes Charon the biggest moon relative to its planet in the entire solar system. In fact, scientists sometimes refer to Pluto and Charon as a double dwarf planet system, rather than calling Charon a moon. So far, scientists don't know of any other double planetary systems in our solar system.

CHARON

NASA's (National Aeronautics and Space Administration) *New Horizons* spacecraft has provided surprising images of canyons, mountains, and landslides on this moon's surface—which scientists had predicted to be covered in impact craters.

SIZE (diameter): 753.1 miles (1,212 km)

PLANET IT ORBITS: Pluto

DISCOVERED: 1978

NAMED FOR: A man in Greek mythology

COSMIC DATA: Charon orbits the dwarf planet Pluto and is about half its size. Charon has mostly been studied by photographs from spacecraft, which was how astronomers James Christy and Robert Harrington discovered this moon. Images show that Charon has a gray color to its surface.

DWARF PLANETS

A dwarf planet is similar to a full planet in structure, but it is too small to be considered a full planet. The difference between a full planet and a dwarf planet can sometimes be hard to figure out—as we well know! Originally considered a full planet, Pluto was demoted to a dwarf planet in 2006, but by 2017, that status was again being questioned.

The definition of a full planet requires the object to orbit the Sun and have enough gravity to be round in shape. The biggest difference between a full planet and a dwarf planet is that a full planet is able to clear its orbit path of other objects. Dwarf planets are so small that their gravity force is not strong enough to push away other planets.

Scientists suggest that there could be up to 200 dwarf planets in our solar system, many of which reside in an area called the Kuiper belt (page 98).

PLUTO

Pluto was named by Venetia Burney, an 11-year-old girl from England! Whether Pluto should be considered a full planet or a dwarf planet is still being debated by people all over the world.

DISTANCE FROM THE SUN: 3.7 billion miles (5.9 billion km)

SIZE (radius): 715 miles (1,151 km)

MOONS: 5

COSMIC DATA: Pluto is an icy planet; it has mountains covered in snow, but the snow is red in color. Pluto also has an intriguing surface—including a heart-shaped crater that's the size of US states Texas and Oklahoma combined. One of Pluto's moons, Charon (page 65), is about half the size of Pluto, which is unusually large for a moon. Pluto was discovered in 1930 and was originally considered the ninth major planet in our solar system. After similar planets were discovered in the Kuiper belt, this small planet was reclassified as a dwarf planet in 2006.

HAUMEA

The two moons that orbit this dwarf planet are named after Haumea's two daughters, **Hi'iaka** and **Namaka**.

DISTANCE FROM THE SUN: 4 billion miles (6 billion km)

SIZE (radius): 385 miles (620 km)

MOONS: 2

COSMIC DATA: Like Eris (page 70), not much is known about Haumea because of its distance from us, but scientists suspect that its surface is made of mostly rock and ice. Discovered in 2003, this dwarf planet is similar in size and location to Pluto. Haumea also resides in the Kuiper belt, beyond the orbit of Neptune. This planet rotates so quickly that its shape is distorted, giving it a football-like appearance. It completes one full rotation in just four Earth hours. Haumea was named for the Hawaiian goddess of fertility, and its moons were named for her two daughters.

MAKEMAKE

Scientists discovered a small object orbiting this planet in 2015, and suspect that it may be a moon.

DISTANCE FROM THE SUN: 4.2 billion miles (6.8 billion km)

SIZE (radius): 444 miles (715 km)

MOONS: 0, 1 provisional

COSMIC DATA: Much like Eris (page 70) and Haumea (page 68), we don't know much about Makemake because it is so far away, but scientific observation suggests that, like Pluto, its surface is made up of ice and rock, and is a reddish brown color. Makemake was discovered in 2005 in the Kuiper belt, and was named for the Rapa Nui (Easter Island) god of fertility.

ERIS

The discovery of Eris was what prompted scientists to first reconsider Pluto's title as a major planet, because the two objects are so similar.

DISTANCE FROM THE SUN: 6.3 billion miles (10.1 billion km)

SIZE (radius): 722 miles (1,163 km)

MOONS: 1

COSMIC DATA: Scientists do not know much about Eris because it is so far away, but it most likely has a rocky surface and extremely cold temperatures like Pluto. Discovered in 2003, this planet is located in the Kuiper belt, and was one of the first to bring up the question of planet versus dwarf planet. Eris was named for the ancient Greek goddess of discord and strife, and its moon is named for her daughter, Dysnomia.

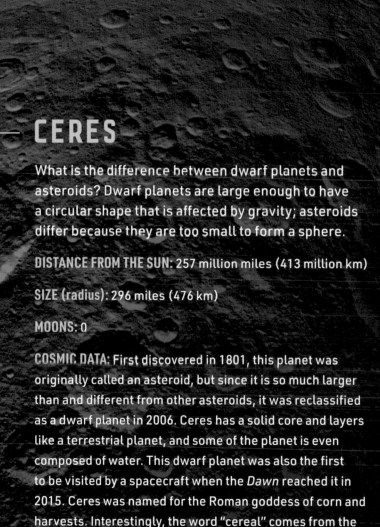

CERES

What is the difference between dwarf planets and asteroids? Dwarf planets are large enough to have a circular shape that is affected by gravity; asteroids differ because they are too small to form a sphere.

DISTANCE FROM THE SUN: 257 million miles (413 million km)

SIZE (radius): 296 miles (476 km)

MOONS: 0

COSMIC DATA: First discovered in 1801, this planet was originally called an asteroid, but since it is so much larger than and different from other asteroids, it was reclassified as a dwarf planet in 2006. Ceres has a solid core and layers like a terrestrial planet, and some of the planet is even composed of water. This dwarf planet was also the first to be visited by a spacecraft when the *Dawn* reached it in 2015. Ceres was named for the Roman goddess of corn and harvests. Interestingly, the word "cereal" comes from the same name!

THE SUN AND OTHER STARS

You might think of a star as a five-pointed yellow object, but stars are actually big balls of gas in the universe. While some stars can be yellow, they can also be red, orange, or blue. A star's color is related to its temperature. Cooler stars are orange or red, and the hottest stars are blue. Stars have a life cycle. They are formed, or born, in giant gas clouds that heat up. The gas falls in on itself, and the star has its own force of gravity to keep that gas together in a ball. Reactions within the ball of gas cause the star to produce heat and light. Stars can shine for billions, or even trillions, of years, but they also eventually die. When a star runs out of the fuel that keeps it burning bright, it explodes and becomes a supernova.

OUR SUN

OTHER NAMES: The Sun is called many different things in different languages.

CONSTELLATION: None

COSMIC DATA: The Sun is a massive yellow dwarf star that sends light and heat into the universe. Unlike the other stars in this chapter, the Sun is visible during the day rather than at night. Without the Sun's energy, we could not have life on Earth. Light from the Sun travels to Earth in about eight minutes. The Sun is about 109 times the size of Earth, and its core has a temperature of 27 million degrees Fahrenheit (15 million degrees Celsius). Scientists estimate that the Sun has only used up about half of its energy, which means it could keep burning for another 5 billion years.

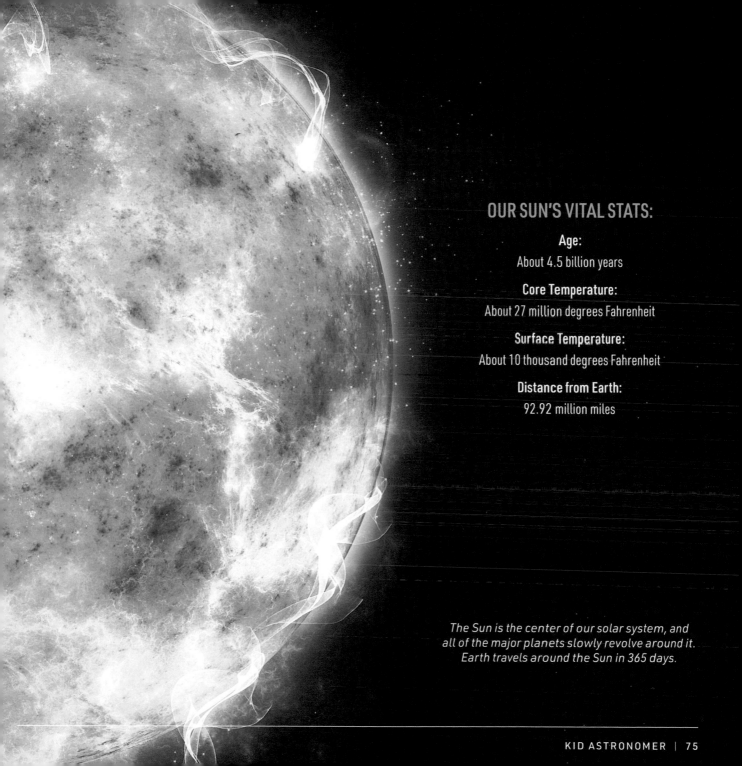

OUR SUN'S VITAL STATS:

Age:

About 4.5 billion years

Core Temperature:

About 27 million degrees Fahrenheit

Surface Temperature:

About 10 thousand degrees Fahrenheit

Distance from Earth:

92.92 million miles

The Sun is the center of our solar system, and all of the major planets slowly revolve around it. Earth travels around the Sun in 365 days.

Polaris is at the very tip of the Ursa Minor constellation...better known as the "Little Dipper."

POLARIS

OTHER NAMES: Alpha Ursae Minoris, the North Star, the Pole Star, the Guiding Star

CONSTELLATION: Ursa Minor

COSMIC DATA: This star has been called the North Star because its location in the sky has allowed it to be used for navigation. Like Alpha Centauri (page 78), Polaris is actually three stars (a trinary star system); one main star has two smaller companion stars near it. It is possible that the North Star may not always be in the same location; Earth's axis moves over thousands of years, and eventually it might move enough to change where we see this star.

SIRIUS

OTHER NAMES: The Dog Star

CONSTELLATION: Canis Major

COSMIC DATA: Sirius appears in the sky as a single bright star, but it's actually two stars together in what's called a binary star system. Sirius A is the brighter of the two stars, and Sirius B is its smaller companion. This star system is actually slowly moving closer to Earth, and scientists expect that it will continue to do so for the next 50–60 thousand years. Don't worry, though. After that, they expect that it will slowly move away from us again. Sirius is also known as the Dog Star because it's the brightest star in the Canis Major, or Big Dog, constellation. The name Sirius actually comes from Ancient Greek, but it recently reappeared in pop culture, thanks to the *Harry Potter* character Sirius Black.

Like the North Star, Sirius has often been used for navigation because it is so bright.

ALPHA CENTAURI

OTHER NAMES: Rigil Kentaurus, Toliman

CONSTELLATION: Centaurus

COSMIC DATA: This star is the third brightest in the night sky, but, like Polaris, it is actually three stars combined in a trinary star system, with one large star and two smaller companions. Mention of this star dates all the way back to English explorer Robert Hues in 1592. There is a planet around one of the Centauri stars, but it is so close to the star that it would be too hot to support life.

The constellation Centaurus gets its name from the centaur, a mythical creature that is half human and half horse.

BETELGEUSE

OTHER NAMES: Alpha Orionis

CONSTELLATION: Orion

COSMIC DATA: Pronounced "beetle-juice," this star was originally named for the Arabic phrase for "hand of Orion," because of the star's central location in the Orion constellation. Right now, this star is one of the largest and brightest in the night sky, but scientists suspect that it will one day die (or "go supernova"), and that the event will be visible from Earth.

This star is also referred to as "the heart of the scorpion," because it is the center of the Scorpius, or scorpion, constellation.

ANTARES

OTHER NAMES: Alpha Scorpii

CONSTELLATION: Scorpius

COSMIC DATA: This star is a red supergiant, and it is so large and bright that it was given the name Antares, or "rival to Mars." Scientists estimate that this star is 850 times larger than our Sun in diameter, and it is 550 million light-years away from Earth. The star is estimated to be 12 million years old, and has been observed by people since ancient times, with mention of it going all the way back to the Ancient Persians in 3000 BCE, when it was believed to be one of four guardian stars of the heavens.

PLEIADES

OTHER NAMES: The Seven Sisters

CONSTELLATION: Taurus

COSMIC DATA: This star is actually a cluster of several stars and is one of the closest star clusters to Earth. The seven largest stars in the cluster are the most visible, giving it the nickname the Seven Sisters, but there are over 1,000 confirmed stars in this cluster. Scientists estimate that the Pleiades is somewhere between 75 million and 150 million years old.

The name for this star cluster comes from ancient Greece. In Greek mythology, the Pleiades were the seven daughters of Atlas, who supposedly held up the night sky.

CONSTELLATIONS

ALL ABOUT ASTERISMS AND CONSTELLATIONS

The Sun is the key to life on Earth and the heart of our solar system. But remember, the Sun is actually much like any other star—and there are countless other stars in the universe! Think of it this way: our home galaxy (the Milky Way galaxy) contains at least 100 billion stars. And the universe might contain 100 billion galaxies. That means billions and billions of stars! Just like our Sun, many stars have their own planets, so the number of worlds in the universe is truly enormous. For thousands of years, humans have looked at the stars and seen asterisms. Asterisms are groups of stars that appear in a pattern, and they are often said to look like images from the mythologies of various cultures around the world. Outside of science, asterisms are often called constellations. Astronomers use the word "constellation" to mean a specific part of the sky, whether or not they're talking about an asterism. Today, astronomers recognize 88 constellations! The asterisms within those constellations are visible in different parts of the world at different times of the year, but most of them can be seen without a telescope. Try looking for some of these asterisms in the night sky where you live!

ARIES

THE RAM

Aries is one of the 12 constellations in the zodiac, which is the part of the sky that the Sun seems to move through over the course of a year. Its name comes from Greek mythology, and it is one of many asterisms that have been recognized by humans since ancient times. Today, Aries is represented as a ram, but it has been interpreted different ways throughout history. Some records indicate that in ancient Egypt, Aries was seen as an image of Amun-Ra—a god who looked like a man with the head of a ram!

CANIS MAJOR

THE BIG DOG

In Latin, Canis Major's name spells out exactly what it represents: a big dog! Specifically, it's said to be one of the two hunting dogs that belong to Orion, the hunter asterism. Canis Major contains **Sirius**, the brightest star in our entire night sky! Sirius, which is also known as the Dog Star, is so bright because it's especially close to our solar system. A star called **VY Canis Majoris**, one of the biggest known stars, is also part of Canis Major.

CANIS MINOR

THE LITTLE DOG

You guessed it: in Latin, Canis Minor means "lesser dog." Like Canis Major, this constellation is usually seen as a hunting dog following Orion. Sometimes, Canis Minor is said to represent a different dog from Greek mythology: Maera, a dog that was legendary for being faithful to its master. **Procyon**, the brightest star in Canis Minor, is also one of the brightest stars in the sky.

CASSIOPEIA

THE QUEEN

Cassiopeia looks like a capital letter W in the northern summer sky. But sometimes the W looks like it's upside down. According to Greek mythology, that's because Cassiopeia was a queen who thought she was more beautiful than the children of the gods. Her punishment for being so vain was to hang upside down some of the time!

CENTAURUS

THE CENTAUR

Centaurus is a centaur—a Greek mythological creature with the body of a horse and the head and chest of a man. Centaurus is home to the **Alpha Centauri** system, which contains the three stars that are our nearest neighbors in the whole universe. The smallest one is closest to our Sun, and it's called **Proxima Centauri**. The stars of Alpha Centauri are hard to see in the Northern Hemisphere, but farther south, they shine very brightly in the summer sky.

LEO

THE LION

Leo is a lion! It has lots of bright stars, so it's often easy to see in the Northern Hemisphere. In particular, the stars that outline the lion's shoulders and mane form a shape that looks like a backward question mark. Leo was recognized by ancient people long before many other asterisms, and many different cultures called it "lion" in their own languages. Leo is another of the constellations in the zodiac. It is also home to a notable meteor shower called the Leonids, which puts on its bright, colorful show each November.

LYRA

THE LYRE

Lyra is said to represent a lyre, which is a small stringed instrument. Lyra is one of the smaller constellations, but also one of the most interesting! It contains **Vega**, which is the fifth-brightest star in the night sky. Other than the Sun, Vega was the first star ever photographed! Lyra is also home to the Ring Nebula, which is a famous planetary nebula. A nebula forms when a star pushes out a bright layer of gas.

ORION

THE HUNTER

For many people, Orion is the star of the stars! It's located right around the equator, which means it can be seen throughout the world. Orion is named after a famed hunter from Greek mythology, and it has been recognized by different names in many cultures throughout recorded history. The three bright stars in a row that often represent the hunter's belt are especially recognizable. Additionally, Orion contains two of the brightest stars in our night sky, **Rigil Kentaurus** and **Betelgeuse**.

URSA MAJOR

THE BIG BEAR

Ursa Major's name in Latin means "great bear," and it lives up to that name—Ursa Major is the third-largest constellation in our entire night sky. Seven of its stars form perhaps the most famous asterism: the **Big Dipper**, which looks like the kind of ladle you might use to serve soup. Sometimes, the Big Dipper is also said to represent other objects, like a plough or a wagon. Ursa Major is also important in navigation, because the tip of the bear's tail (or the handle of the ladle!) points toward the **North Star**.

URSA MINOR

THE LITTLE BEAR

Ursa Minor is the "little bear" to Ursa Major's "great bear," and it also has a group of stars that looks like a ladle. Those stars are known as the **Little Dipper**. Ursa Minor is much smaller than Ursa Major, but it's just as important: its brightest star is **Polaris**, which is also known as the North Star. Polaris is actually a system of three stars close together, and they're known as the North Star because they're in the part of the sky that's right above Earth's North Pole. Especially for sailors (or anyone trying to figure out directions!), finding Polaris is one sure way of knowing which way is north.

GALAXIES

Galaxies are structures in the universe where stars are formed. They are made up of dust, stars, and gas held together by gravity, and can contain objects like planets. Some galaxies have large black holes at their center.

There are three basic types of galaxies: spiral, elliptical, and irregular. Spiral galaxies are the most common, and have long arms coming out from the center that make a shape like a pinwheel. Elliptical galaxies are flat, smooth galaxies in the shape of an oval. Irregular galaxies are the least common type, and include any galaxies that are not spirals or ovals; they typically have a blob-like shape.

Scientists don't know how many galaxies there are in the universe, but they estimate that there could be billions. Sometimes, galaxies get close enough to each other that they overlap, or even collide to form new galaxies.

THE MILKY WAY

As of yet, scientists are not able to obtain actual images of the Milky Way from outside the galaxy...but by studying the parts that can be seen from Earth, as well as other galaxies, astronomers have been able to learn enough about the Milky Way to produce pictures of what it most likely looks like from space.

TYPE: Spiral

CONSTELLATION: Orion and Sagittarius

TRUE NAME: This galaxy has many names in many languages.

COSMIC DATA: The Milky Way galaxy is of great interest to scientists because it is our home galaxy. Although it's hard to see something that our planet is actually inside of, on a clear night there are bands of light across the sky, which is our Earth's view of the Milky Way. Our galaxy is estimated to be about 100,000 light-years in size, and is surrounded by gas in the shape of a halo that makes it even larger. The Milky Way also has a large black hole at its center. If you could look at the Milky Way from above, it would look like it has a bar across the center. This bar is made up of gas and stars, and it is the reason why the Milky Way's spiral is called a barred spiral. The Milky Way contains billions of stars, the most common type being the red dwarf star. Our solar system, including the Sun and the major planets, is located in the area of the Milky Way called the Orion Arm.

ANDROMEDA

Andromeda may be our neighbor, but even though it is the nearest galaxy to the Milky Way, it is still over two million light-years away!

TYPE: Spiral

CONSTELLATION: Andromeda

TRUE NAME: M31

COSMIC DATA: The Andromeda galaxy is our nearest neighboring galaxy, and sometimes it's so close to us that we can see it on a clear night. It looks like a hazy patch or smudge in the sky. Scientists have been able to take pictures of this galaxy with the Hubble Space Telescope (page 114). In size, the Andromeda galaxy is similar to the Milky Way. In fact, this galaxy is slowly moving closer to us, and scientists estimate that eventually the Milky Way and Andromeda will merge and create a new, combined galaxy. Don't worry, though. They don't think this will happen for another 4–6 billion years.

CENTAURUS A

Centaurus A is an elliptical-type galaxy because of its long, flat oval shape.

TYPE: Elliptical

CONSTELLATION: Centaurus

TRUE NAME: NGC 5128

COSMIC DATA: Centaurus A is unusual because its shape is slightly warped, making it look like it has elements of a spiral galaxy. Scientists suspect that this active galaxy may be the result of a collision of two other galaxies millions of years ago. Centaurus A is about 11–12 million light-years from Earth.

THE SOMBRERO GALAXY

Sombrero is a Spanish word that refers to a type of hat, giving this galaxy its name.

TYPE: Elliptical

CONSTELLATION: Virgo

TRUE NAME: M104

COSMIC DATA: The Hubble Space Telescope has taken pictures of the Sombrero galaxy that show it has a long, flat shape with an unusually large bulge of stars near its center—giving it the appearance of a hat. Scientists think that the center of this galaxy may be a massive black hole. While not visible to the naked eye, the Sombrero Galaxy can be seen from Earth with the help of small telescopes at certain times of the year. It was first discovered in 1781.

THE WHIRLPOOL GALAXY

The Whirlpool galaxy is a perfect example of a spiral-type galaxy, because each of its arms is so clearly visible.

TYPE: Spiral

CONSTELLATION: Canes Venatici

TRUE NAME: M51

COSMIC DATA: Discovered in 1773, the Whirlpool galaxy has since been photographed with the Hubble Space Telescope. This galaxy's well-defined arms are the source of its nickname. These arms are star formation zones; scientists think they may be so visible because a nearby galaxy has such a strong tidal force that it is causing more stars to form within the arms.

THE ANTENNAE GALAXIES

The Antennae galaxies will not always look like this, because the two galaxies that form this pair are slowly merging together and changing shape.

TYPE: Spiral

CONSTELLATION: Corvus

TRUE NAME: NGC 4038 and NGC 4039

COSMIC DATA: The Antennae galaxies are actually a pair of spiral galaxies that are linked together. These two galaxies have been colliding for hundreds of millions of years; the impacts are so strong that stars and gas have been flung from the galaxies, creating long, antennae-like streamers between the two. Eventually, these two galaxies will fully combine to become one galaxy.

THE PINWHEEL GALAXY

The arms of spiral galaxies are usually the regions where new stars are formed. Information from four NASA telescopes shows that there are equal amounts of old and new stars in the Pinwheel's arms.

TYPE: Spiral

CONSTELLATION: Ursa Major

TRUE NAME: M101

COSMIC DATA: This galaxy's spiral arms are very well defined, thus giving it the appearance of a pinwheel. Scientists do not think that this galaxy has a black hole at its center, which is unusual. The Pinwheel galaxy contains about 3,000 "starbirth" regions (star formation areas), which is the most of any observed galaxies of this type.

ASTEROIDS, COMETS, METEORS, AND MORE

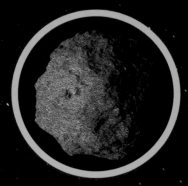

101955 Bennu

ASTEROIDS

ANCIENT ARTIFACTS AND COSMIC SNOWBALLS

Asteroids are bits of rock that have been around since our solar system formed over four billion years ago. Comets—which some scientists call "cosmic snowballs"—are clumps of space dust and gas that start to burn when they get close to the Sun.

Eros

There are almost one million known asteroids so far, and most of them are part of a giant asteroid belt that orbits the Sun between Mars and Jupiter. Asteroids come in lots of different sizes, from ones that could fit in your house to ones hundreds of miles in diameter. Scientists often study specific asteroids. For instance, scientists have sent a spacecraft to an asteroid called 101955 Bennu, where it will gather samples that could give us insight into the history of life on Earth. Bennu got its name in 2013, but not from scientists—it was named by a nine-year-old who won a contest!

Vesta

COMETS

As comets orbit the Sun, burning gas and dust fly off them, making beautiful tails that we can sometimes see in the sky. There are over 3,000 comets identified so far.

- Halley's Comet passes close enough to see from Earth about once every 75 years. Historical records show observations of Halley's Comet dating back more than 2,000 years.

- 'Oumuamua was the first confirmed interstellar visitor to our solar system—that means it originally came from a different star! Its name is a Hawaiian word that means "a messenger from afar arriving first."

- 19P/Borrelly looks just like a chicken leg!

Halley's Comet

METEOROIDS, METEORS, AND METEORITES

SPACE ROCKS

These three kinds of space rocks are actually all the same space rocks— just at different times! Here's how to tell the difference between them:

Meteoroids are essentially rocks floating in space, whether tiny or large.

Sometimes, meteoroids fly through a planet's atmosphere and burn up, which makes them **meteors**—also called fireballs or shooting stars.

If a meteor makes it all the way to the surface of the planet, then it becomes a **meteorite**!

'Oumuamua

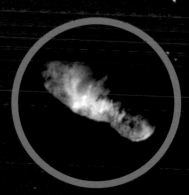

19P/Borrelly

THE KUIPER BELT

The Kuiper belt is a doughnut-shaped region in our solar system that is very far away from Earth. It's located way out past Neptune, and it's full of ancient, icy objects of many different shapes and sizes—from tiny comets to dwarf planets! The dwarf planets Pluto, Haumea, Makemake, and Eris are all in the Kuiper belt. The Kuiper belt is also home to a small, icy space object named Arrokoth that looks like a red snowman, which scientists learned about when the spacecraft *New Horizons* flew by it in 2019. Arrokoth's name comes from a Native American word that means "sky" in the Powhatan/Algonquian language—which makes sense, since it's the farthest-away object that humans have ever explored up close!

Mercury

Venus

Earth

Mars

Jupiter

Saturn

Uranus

Neptune

THE OORT CLOUD

The Oort cloud is even farther away from Earth than the Kuiper belt. It's all the way at the far edge of our solar system, and it's thought to be shaped like a giant bubble that creates a shell around the entire solar system. No spacecraft from Earth have ever visited the Oort cloud, so scientists have never looked at it directly. Instead, scientists have learned about the Oort cloud from comets that seem to have come from it.

The Oort cloud is made up of countless icy objects, some as big as mountains—or bigger! And the Oort cloud is so far away that even the spacecraft *Voyager 1*— which travels about one million miles every day!—won't reach the closest edge of the Oort cloud for at least 300 years.

DARK MATTER

Dark matter is one of space's greatest mysteries. No one yet knows exactly what it is, it's invisible, and scientists haven't been able to study it directly. So how do we know it exists? The answer is complex, but essentially scientists studied certain aspects of the universe—including the gravity that pulls on light from faraway stars, the movements of galaxies, and particular kinds of radiation—and realized that there must be much more mass in the universe than what we can observe directly. It's a little bit like looking at the shadow of something and trying to figure out what that thing is! All that extra mass is dark matter. Even though we don't know what it is, scientists estimate that dark matter makes up about **27%** of the universe.

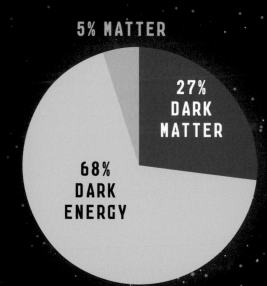

5% MATTER

27% DARK MATTER

68% DARK ENERGY

Some scientists have theories about what dark matter might be. A few possibilities include:

Brown dwarfs, which are stars that never became big enough to start burning

White dwarfs, which are leftover cores from dead stars

Black holes or **neutron stars**, which are left when especially large stars explode

Something else altogether! It could be that dark matter is made of particles that scientists don't even know about yet.

There's also another mystery called **dark energy**. We know about the existence of dark energy because images from the Hubble Space Telescope (page 114) revealed that the universe is expanding faster all the time—we just don't know why that is. Whatever is causing the universe to expand is what scientists call dark energy. Scientists think that dark energy might make up as much as 68% of the universe. That means that matter we can observe—planets, moons, stars, and nearly everything mentioned in this book—is really only about 5% of what the universe contains.

SUPERLATIVES

The universe is made up of objects big and small, and each one is unique. Planets, moons, stars, asteroids, and meteors all vary in size and shape, and scientists have noted some particularly interesting discoveries. Some of these unique space objects, like the Veil Nebula (page 105), Hoba meteorite (page 106), and star Deneb (page 104) can be seen from Earth. Space technology has also allowed us to look at distant objects more closely and learn about what makes them special. The universe is so vast that every object could be considered unique in some way, but these are a few of the most notable objects in (or from) outer space.

Comet McNaught, also known as C/2006 P1, was discovered by Robert H. McNaught on August 7, 2006. It was the brightest comet seen from Earth in decades.

COMET MCNAUGHT

SUPERLATIVE: Biggest comet

TAIL SIZE: 35 degrees long

COSMIC DATA: Comet McNaught—also known as "The Great Comet of 2007"—was spectacular in a variety of ways. Not only did it have an incredibly long tail, but it was also so bright that it was sometimes visible during the day. But what made this comet the biggest was not just its size, but also how it disturbed the space around it. The longer it takes spacecraft to get through the disturbed area, the bigger the comet's impact. The spacecraft *Ulysses* took 18 days to pass through the area disturbed by the comet. That's a long time! For comparison, the same spacecraft went through the wake of another large comet in just 2.5 days.

DENEB

Deneb is a blue supergiant, which means this star is hundreds of times larger (and much hotter!) than our Sun.

SUPERLATIVE: Farthest visible star

CONSTELLATION: Cygnus

COSMIC DATA: Scientists estimate that the star Deneb could be anywhere from 2,000 to 7,000 light-years away, but they aren't sure. What they do know is that while the distance is incredibly far, Deneb is still visible in the night sky as part of the constellation Cygnus. Scientists think that this is the farthest star from Earth that can be seen in the night sky without the help of a telescope. The star's name is from the Arabic word for "tail" and part of the phrase for "the hen's tail." Although the constellation Cygnus is now called the Swan, it also used to be thought of as a chicken.

THE VEIL NEBULA

This famous supernova is 110 light-years across at its widest point, and is located over 2,100 light-years from Earth.

SUPERLATIVE: Best-known supernova

EXPLODED: 8,000 years ago

COSMIC DATA: A supernova is what happens when a star dies out and explodes; the Veil Nebula is the wispy debris from one of these explosions. This nebula is so well known not only for its delicate structure, but also because it is visible from Earth in the constellation Cygnus. The Hubble Space Telescope (page 114) was able to take images of this nebula, and scientists have estimated that the remains are of a star that was 20 times more massive than our Sun.

HOBA METEORITE

Because 71% of Earth's surface is made up of water, many meteorites land in deep seawater.

SUPERLATIVE: Largest meteorite

SIZE: 9 feet (2.7 m)

COSMIC DATA: Chunks of meteors sometimes make their way through Earth's atmosphere and land on the ground as meteorites. Some meteorites are tiny—but sometimes they reach Earth as large chunks. The Hoba meteorite was discovered in 1920 by a farmer in Namibia, and is the largest meteorite to hit Earth. The Hoba is made up of iron and nickel, and its weight is estimated to be about 60 tons. If you take a trip to Grootfontein, Namibia, you can even see this meteorite up close.

2015 TC25

Scientists used four separate telescopes to study this asteroid as it flew by Earth in October 2015.

SUPERLATIVE: Smallest asteroid

SIZE: 6 feet (2 m)

COSMIC DATA: Asteroids are any small, rocky objects orbiting the Sun, and they can range in size. The smallest ever studied is the 2015 TC25. This asteroid is a solid chunk of rock that, for an asteroid, spins incredibly fast—one rotation every two minutes. This asteroid flew by Earth in 2015, giving us the opportunity to study it. What also sets this asteroid apart is the lack of dirt or dust on it; because of this, 2015 TC25 has been nicknamed a "bald" asteroid.

SPACE TECHNOLOGY

Outer space is so big and wide that it is impossible to see everything contained in it from Earth. Since the invention of the telescope in the early 1600s, scientists have been looking for new ways to explore space.

With the high-tech cameras and equipment that are now available, space technology has become very advanced. Spacecraft are machines that can be anything from small probes to huge space shuttles. Sometimes they're robots that head out on their own, and sometimes they're vehicles that carry astronauts inside them! Usually, spacecraft need rockets to launch them into space. Some types of spacecraft just observe and monitor planets, while others can actually land and explore them. Today's space technology makes it possible for humans to travel to and live in outer space!

ROCKETS

When it comes to exploring space, rockets do the heavy lifting. They burn powerful fuel to launch all kinds of things into space—including satellites, supplies for the **International Space Station** (page 119), and spacecraft heading out to explore other worlds. Rockets also launch astronauts into space during NASA missions! Usually, rockets create clouds of gas when they burn fuel, and that gas is what pushes the rockets forward through space.

MARINER 4

MISSION: Conduct a flyby of Mars and take photographs

LAUNCHED: 1965

PLANETARY DATA: The *Mariner 4* was one in a series of 10 spacecraft sent to record information from Mercury, Venus, and Mars. The *Mariner 4* provided NASA with the first up-close pictures of Mars and paved the way for future Mariner missions.

PIONEER 10 AND PIONEER 11

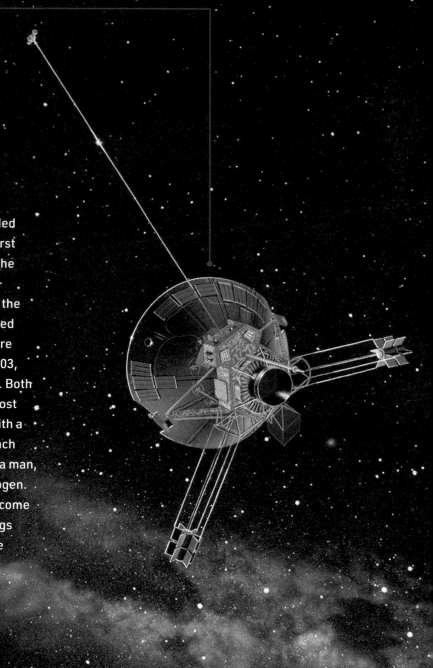

Pioneer 10 and *Pioneer 11* were the first two spacecraft to ever leave our solar system; scientists do not know if the spacecraft are still transmitting signals.

MISSION: Explore Jupiter

LAUNCHED: 1973

COSMIC DATA: This pair of spacecraft far exceeded their mission to explore Jupiter and were the first to reach the planet. *Pioneer 10* took images of the planet and collected scientific data on its atmosphere. *Pioneer 11* went past Jupiter and made the first observations of Saturn. Both missions ended when communications with both spacecraft were lost. The last signal from *Pioneer 10* came in 2003, and the last signal from *Pioneer 11* was in 1995. Both will continue to float through outer space as ghost ships...until they are destroyed by a collision with a star or planet. A gold plaque was attached to each spacecraft; these plaques showed drawings of a man, a woman, and the symbol for the element hydrogen. If either of the *Pioneer* spacecraft happened to come into contact with other life forms, these drawings would be our message to them. The plaques are referred to as the *Pioneer* plaques.

VIKING 1 AND VIKING 2

MISSION: Land a spacecraft on the surface of Mars

LAUNCHED: 1976

PLANETARY DATA: The *Viking 1* and *Viking 2* orbiter and lander spacecraft became the first to land on the surface of Mars. Viking 1 landed first on July 20, 1976, followed by *Viking 2* on September 3, 1976. Both spacecraft conducted biological experiments to try to detect signs of life on Mars. While they did not find any signs of life, they did find valuable information about the surface of Mars.

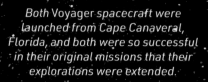

VOYAGER 1 AND VOYAGER 2

MISSION: Explore Jupiter and Saturn

LAUNCHED: 1977

COSMIC DATA: *Voyager 1* and *Voyager 2* are robotic probes that NASA originally sent to explore Jupiter and Saturn, but they didn't stop there! They made the exciting discovery of volcanoes on Io and explored Saturn's rings. They've both been flying through space for over 40 years, and they still send data about the far reaches of space back to scientists on Earth. *Voyager 1* made history as the first spacecraft to reach interstellar space—which is what the area between stars is called. *Voyager 2* flew by Uranus and Neptune; it's the only spacecraft that has ever visited those far-off worlds.

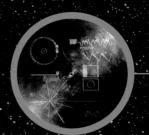

The Golden Record consists of 115 images, 12 minutes of a variety of natural sounds, 90 minutes of musical selections from different cultures and eras, and spoken greetings from Earth-people in 55 languages.

Today, both *Voyager 1* and *Voyager 2* are exploring interstellar space at the far edges of our solar system, and they're both over 10 billion miles from the Sun.

The *Voyager* probes won't ever return to Earth. But, using a giant radio system called the Deep Space Network, they have sent all kinds of important information back to Earth. Both *Voyager 1* and *Voyager 2* carry copies of what's called the Golden Record, which is a record holding music and sounds from Earth, as well as pictures and scientific data about our home. If the *Voyager* probes ever run into any alien civilizations, the records will be our message of life on Earth!

HUBBLE SPACE TELESCOPE

This enormous space telescope is named for astronomer Edwin Hubble, who used the largest telescope in existence in the 1920s to explore space.

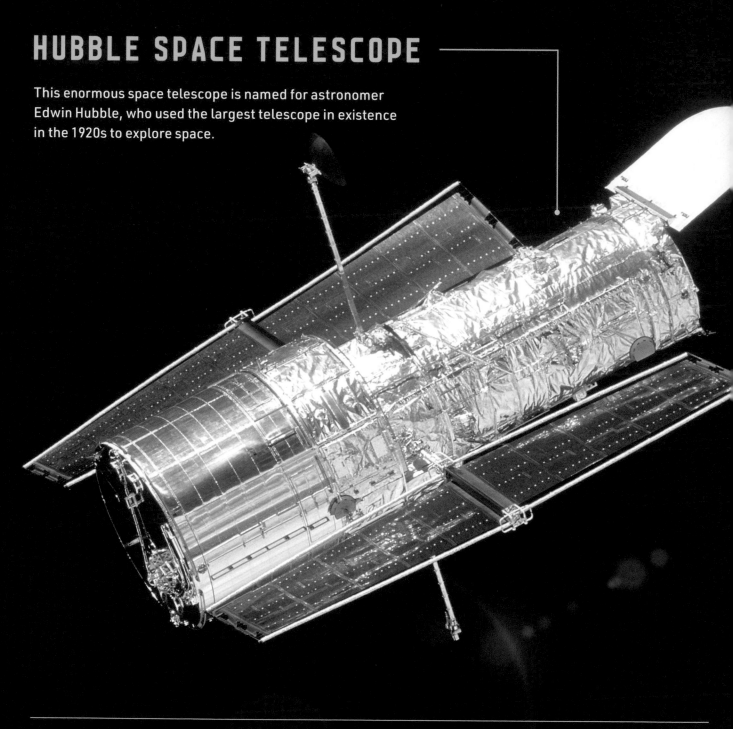

MISSION: Observe space

LAUNCHED: 1990

COSMIC DATA: The Hubble Space Telescope was the first major telescope to be placed in space, and it has permanently changed our ability to view space. The telescope has been in operation since being launched, thanks to servicing missions to keep it functioning. It is approximately the length of a school bus and weighs about 27,000 pounds. Hubble travels around Earth at 17,000 mph to take pictures of space and has made more than one million observations. Some of the images Hubble has made are of galaxies billions of light-years away! That means that the light from those galaxies took billions of years to reach Hubble. NASA launched Hubble in 1990, and today it's used by astronomers all over the world to study our universe. Hubble has taught us so much of what we know about space: it has shown us images of countless faraway galaxies, helped scientists discover dark energy, and provided evidence that the universe is over 13 billion years old. Who knows what Hubble might reveal in the future!

MARS PATHFINDER

Information from the Pathfinder mission suggests that at some point, Mars was a warm planet with water sources.

MISSION: Be the first robotic rover to land on Mars

LAUNCHED: 1996

COSMIC DATA: The *Mars Pathfinder* only explored Mars for a few months, but it accomplished its mission of being the first rover to land on the planet; this paved the way for future exploration efforts—like the Mars rovers *Opportunity* and *Spirit* (page 120). The *Pathfinder* was equipped with instruments to study both the atmosphere and soil of the planet. This spacecraft had an innovative way of landing on the planet, using technology that included a parachute and huge airbags.

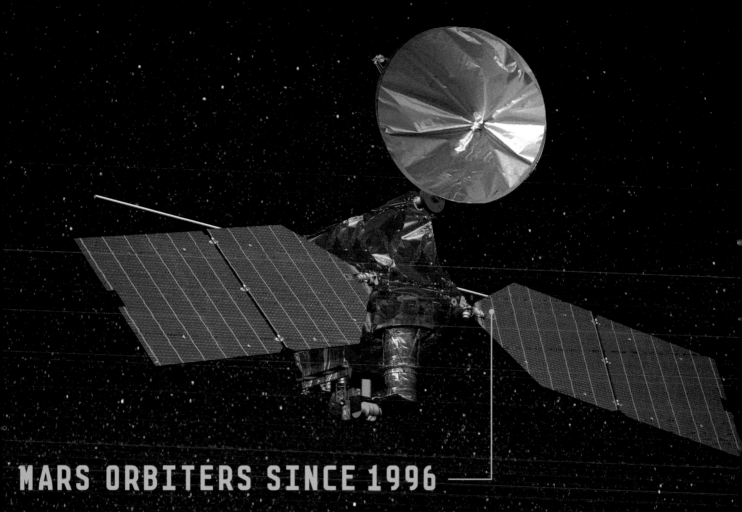

MARS ORBITERS SINCE 1996

In 1996, NASA launched Mars Global Surveyor, the first successful US mission to Mars since the Viking missions in 1976. Since then, many spacecraft have been sent by the United States, Europe, and other countries to orbit Mars. They have provided us with an enormous amount of data that has revolutionized our knowledge of the Red Planet. These missions sent back in-depth information on the topography, atmosphere, geology, mineralogy, water content, and internal structure of Mars. They have allowed scientists to produce detailed maps of Mars, create 3-D models of its relief, and even see under its surface. Images from the HiRISE camera on the *Mars Reconnaissance Orbiter*, launched in 2003, show us details as small as a coffee table on the Martian surface, so we can even produce 3-D models of these features!

CASSINI SPACECRAFT

MISSION: Observe Saturn

LAUNCHED: 1997

COSMIC DATA: *Cassini* was a spacecraft that NASA (working with scientists in Europe) sent into orbit around Saturn. *Cassini* orbited Saturn for more than 10 years and sent scientists tons of data about Saturn, its rings, and its many moons. It also brought along a probe called *Huygens*, which it dropped onto Titan, Saturn's largest moon. *Huygens*'s landing was the first time that humans ever landed an object on a moon other than Earth's moon! The images that *Cassini* sent back to Earth are some of the most stunning pictures of our solar system. In 2017, the mission ended when *Cassini* left Saturn's orbit and burned up in the planet's atmosphere, which scientists had planned so that *Cassini* would not hit any of Saturn's moons when it ran out of fuel.

INTERNATIONAL SPACE STATION

The International Space Station has two bathrooms, five bedrooms, and a gym. It is as big as an entire football field.

MISSION: Provide a lab and home for astronauts in space

LAUNCHED: 1998

COSMIC DATA: The International Space Station is a livable space station created in a collaboration among 15 different nations, and it is the largest object humans have ever put in space. While construction on the space station wasn't finished until 2011, it has been continuously occupied since 2000. More than 230 people from 18 different countries have lived there, but it generally only has three to six people on it at a time. The International Space Station circles Earth every 90 minutes. You can track its location online, but it is also sometimes visible in the night sky—without a telescope—because the station is so reflective.

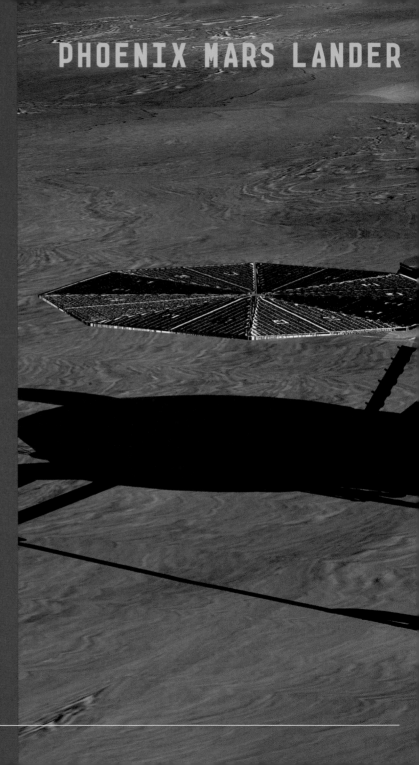

OPPORTUNITY AND SPIRIT

MISSION: Explore Mars

LAUNCHED: 2003

PLANETARY DATA: *Opportunity* and *Spirit* are twin spacecraft that NASA launched to explore Mars. They're both rovers, which means that they're robots that drive around on the surface of Mars! *Spirit* got stuck in Martian dirt and ended its mission in 2011, and NASA stayed in touch with *Opportunity* all the way until 2018, when a dust storm blocked communications. During their time exploring Mars, *Opportunity* and *Spirit* sent back huge amounts of information to NASA, including evidence that Mars seemed to have liquid water a long time ago and could have supported life as we know it. Both rovers have mounted cameras and a robotic arm that works much like a human arm. These features allowed the rovers to take panoramic images of the planet, as well as samples of the planet's surface.

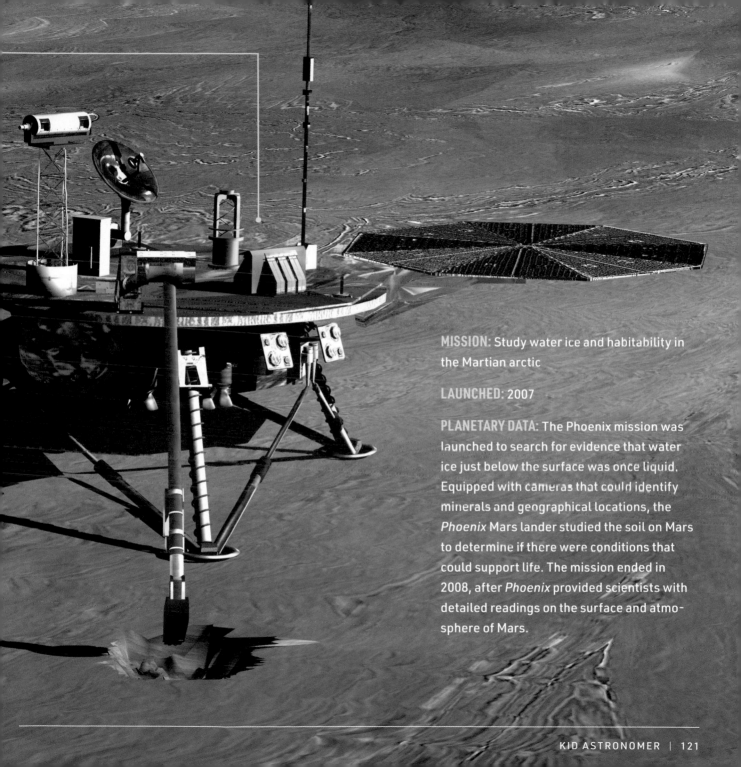

MISSION: Study water ice and habitability in the Martian arctic

LAUNCHED: 2007

PLANETARY DATA: The Phoenix mission was launched to search for evidence that water ice just below the surface was once liquid. Equipped with cameras that could identify minerals and geographical locations, the *Phoenix* Mars lander studied the soil on Mars to determine if there were conditions that could support life. The mission ended in 2008, after *Phoenix* provided scientists with detailed readings on the surface and atmosphere of Mars.

CURIOSITY

MISSION: Study the habitability of Mars

LAUNCHED: 2012

PLANETARY DATA: The *Curiosity* rover landed on Mars on August 6, 2012, to analyze rock and dirt samples and evaluate whether the environment was capable of supporting microbial life. Outfitted with a solar power supply and the ability to travel an average of 98 feet (30 m) per hour, *Curiosity* has since traveled over 6 miles (10 km) and is still functioning. *Curiosity* drills rocks, analyzes samples, and has even taken a Mars selfie!

Every year on August 5, the *Curiosity* rover sings itself "Happy Birthday" to commemorate its landing on the surface of the planet.

INSIGHT LANDER

MISSION: Explore Mars's deep interior

LAUNCHED: 2018

PLANETARY DATA: *InSight* has placed a seismometer on the surface of Mars to measure seismic activity (or marsquakes) and provide information on Mars's interior structure. *InSight*'s seismometer has been detecting new marsquakes every day and has allowed researchers to create the first-ever map of the interior of another planet! It revealed that the crust of Mars (its topmost layer) is between 12 and 23 miles (20 to 37 km) thick, and the underlying mantle (the layer under the crust but above the central core) extends 970 miles (1,561 km) down to the core of the planet. The core of Mars is also bigger (1,137 miles, or 1,830 km, in radius) and has more liquid than scientists expected. Learning about the interior structure of Mars could bring a new understanding of the formation and evolution of terrestrial planets like Earth.

PERSEVERANCE ROVER

MISSION: Search for evidence of ancient life at the surface of Mars, and collect rock and soil samples to be returned to Earth in the future

LAUNCHED: 2020

PLANETARY DATA: The *Perseverance* rover landed on Mars on February 18, 2021, in Jezero Crater. This landing site was chosen because images from orbit showed that it contains an ancient river delta. A very long time ago, Jezero Crater probably contained a lake. The sediments that are deposited in river deltas and lakes are known to preserve signs of life over long periods of time. Therefore, *Perseverance*'s landing site is a very good place to look for signs of ancient microbial life on Mars. To accomplish its mission, the rover will use its many instruments to analyze the rocks and the surrounding atmosphere.

INGENUITY HELICOPTER

Perseverance did not land alone on Mars. It carried on its belly a small helicopter called *Ingenuity*. The first objective of *Ingenuity* was to demonstrate that it is possible to fly a remote-controlled aircraft on Mars. Such a flight had never been attempted before! On April 19, 2021, *Ingenuity* made history by completing its first flight on the Red Planet, taking off vertically, hovering 9.8 feet (3 m) above the surface, and landing after 39 seconds. Since then, it has completed several other flights, higher and longer than the first one. These flights are used to test how such an aircraft can help us better explore Mars and other planets in the future.

FUTURE MISSIONS

NASA and other space agencies are always working on sending new probes and space-craft to Mars, to help discover more about the surface of the Red Planet and to help prepare for a manned Mars mission. The launch of the *Perseverance* rover is the first phase of an ambitious mission to return samples of the Martian ground to Earth.

FUTURE SAMPLE RETURN MISSION

Rovers are able to perform very advanced analyses of Martian rocks. However, some types of studies can only be performed by scientists on Earth. For that reason, NASA is planning to bring back some of the Martian rocks to Earth. Whenever the *Perseverance* rover finds particularly interesting rocks or sediments, it stores a sample in a little tube and leaves the tube at the surface of Mars. In 2026, another rover will retrieve the samples, and a rocket will launch them into the orbit of Mars. In 2028, a new spacecraft will recover the samples in orbit, and then return to Earth in 2031. The samples will then be analyzed directly by scientists in laboratories on Earth. Those analyses will hopefully lead to new and exciting discoveries about Mars!

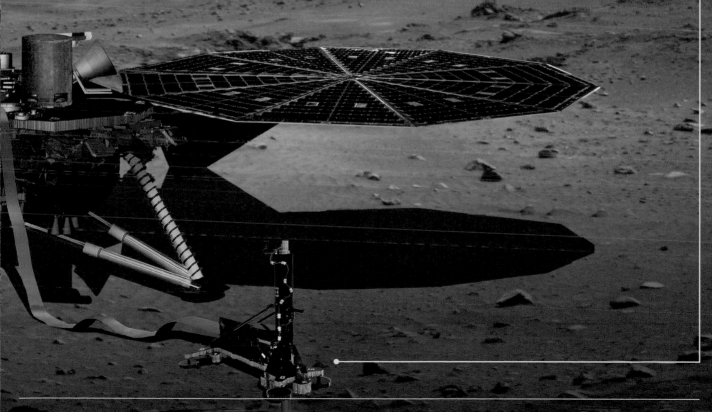

LOOKING FOR LIFE OUT THERE

Given how enormous the universe is, lots of scientists think that there must be life of some kind beyond Earth. That's right—aliens could be real! But if they are, what are they like? Where are they, and how do we find them? These are questions that scientists are working hard to answer. Right now, tools like the Hubble Space Telescope (page 114) and probes exploring the far reaches of space are looking for information about any signs of life that might be out there.

When scientists talk about finding life, they often mean finding what's called "life as we know it"—that is, creatures that have cells and that rely on familiar things like water and oxygen in order to survive. In other words, creatures a lot like the living things on Earth! But it's also possible that space could hold life as we don't know it. It could be that in faraway worlds, life has evolved in ways that we can't even imagine. So if we do find alien life, it might not look anything like we've ever expected!

RIGHT NOW, SCIENTISTS ARE FOCUSING ON A FEW LIKELY TARGETS IN THE SEARCH FOR LIFE BEYOND EARTH:

Mars: Our neighboring planet probably doesn't hold any life today. But living things may have lived there in the past, since there's some evidence that there used to be liquid water on Mars. NASA has plans to launch a new rover to look for more evidence—and maybe even alien fossils!

Europa: Because Jupiter's moon Europa probably has an ocean of liquid water underneath its icy surface, it's one of the places most likely to be home to life as we know it. Within the next few years, NASA will launch a new spacecraft called the *Europa Clipper* to explore Europa further! Titan, Saturn's biggest moon, is another possibility for finding signs of life in our solar system.

Exoplanets: Exoplanets are planets that orbit other stars rather than our own Sun. There are hundreds of billions of exoplanets in the Milky Way, our home galaxy, so scientists are working on building powerful telescopes that can fly to outer space and search those distant worlds for signs of life! One of them, the James Webb Space Telescope, was launched on December 25, 2021.

THE APOLLO PROGRAM

The Apollo program was NASA's first program for sending humans to the Moon! The first Apollo flight was in 1968 and the last one was in 1972. The earlier flights tested the spacecraft and other equipment, and the later flights carried astronauts to the Moon. The astronauts rode in a spacecraft called the Apollo Command Module, and they used another space-craft, the Lunar Module, to land on the Moon once they got there. Apollo 11 in July 1969 was the first mission in all of human history to land on the Moon. During the Apollo program, 12 astronauts in total walked on the Moon. They studied what they saw and brought samples of Moon rocks back to Earth for the first time!

Astronaut Buzz Aldrin and the Apollo 11 Lunar Module, Eagle, on the surface of the Moon, July 20, 1969, as photographed by Mission Commander Neil Armstrong.

THE BEGINNINGS OF SPACE EXPLORATION

October 4, 1957: The Union of Soviet Socialist Republics (USSR) launches Sputnik 1, the first artificial Earth satellite.

January 31, 1958: The United States launches the Explorer 1 satellite.

October 11, 1958: NASA launches Pioneer 1, weighing only 84 lbs. (38 kg), to measure cosmic radiation between Earth and the Moon.

April 12, 1961: Russian cosmonaut Yuri Gagarin becomes the first man in space.

May 25, 1961: President Kennedy calls for the United States to put a man on the Moon before the end of the decade.

July 31, 1964: After 13 failed missions, the United States has its first success with the Ranger 7, providing detailed photos of the Moon's surface.

NASA

After the Union of Soviet Socialist Republics (USSR) successfully launched the first satellite, Sputnik 1, on October 4, 1957, the United States decided to put its full effort toward exploring space.

While the first US satellite—the Explorer 1, launched on January 31, 1958—was not helmed by NASA, its success sparked the space craze during the '60s. NASA (National Aeronautics and Space Administration) was founded on July 29, 1958, with the passing of the National Aeronautics and Space Act of 1958.

When NASA first started, it had only 8,000 employees. The first NASA mission was October 11, 1958, with the launch of Pioneer 1 that paved the way for NASA's future of space exploration and discovery.

The Space Race was a time period in history during which the United States and the USSR raced to see who could place a man on the Moon first. The USSR started the race by launching Sputnik 1 into orbit. With the founding of NASA, the United States dove into the race. The United States became the first country to place a man on the surface of the Moon in 1969, with the success of the Apollo 11 mission.

February 3, 1966: The USSR's unmanned Luna 9 has the first soft landing on the Moon.

June 2, 1966: The United States' Surveyor 1 completes a soft Moon landing.

December 24, 1968: The US crew of Apollo 8 becomes the first humans to orbit the Moon.

July 20, 1969: The Apollo 11 crew lands on the surface of the Moon. The United States becomes the first nation to put a man on the Moon!

The launch of the beach ball–sized Sputnik is widely regarded as the beginning of the Space Age. The Russian word "Sputnik" means "companion" (or "satellite," in the astronomical sense). The United Nations has designated the first week of October as "World Space Week" to celebrate humanity's achievements in space science and technology.

PROJECT APOLLO:
MISSIONS TIME LINE

Named after the Greek god of the sun, Project Apollo (or the "Apollo missions") was developed to further lunar exploration. From Apollo 1, named to honor the brave astronauts who did not get to carry out their mission, to the last manned mission to the Moon, Apollo 17, Project Apollo brought a greater understanding of space, space travel, and the surface of the Moon.

APOLLO 8
DECEMBER 21 TO 27, 1968

The first mission that took humans to the Moon, the Apollo 8 crew completed eight orbits around the Moon and broadcast the first up-close images of its surface.

APOLLO 10
MAY 18 TO 26, 1969

Apollo 10 was the "dress rehearsal" for the Apollo 11 mission, and included all of the steps for the lunar landing without actually landing on the surface. It was the first mission to fly with the entire Apollo spacecraft configuration that would be used in future missions.

APOLLO 1
JANUARY 27, 1967

Scheduled to launch on February 21, 1967, as the first manned Project Apollo mission, the AS-204 mission came to a tragic end on January 27, 1967, when a Command Module fire during a launch pad test killed all three crew members. It was forever immortalized as Apollo 1 in memory of its brave crew.

APOLLO 7
OCTOBER 11 TO 22, 1968

The first successful manned Apollo mission, the crew of Apollo 7 orbited Earth 163 times and spent 10 days and 20 hours in space.

APOLLO 9
MARCH 3 TO 13, 1969

A manned planning mission, Apollo 9 functioned as a test mission to ensure that future lunar landing attempts would be successful, including docking and repair techniques.

APOLLO 11
JULY 16 TO 24, 1969

The first successful lunar landing mission in history, Apollo
11 ended the Space Race and
completed President John F.
Kennedy's goal of placing a man
on the Moon before the end of
the decade.

APOLLO 13
APRIL 11 TO 17, 1970

Due to an oxygen tank explosion,
this lunar landing mission turned
into a survival mission, as the
Command Module lost the ability
to produce electricity, water, and
oxygen. The crew survived by stay-
ing in the Lunar Module and they
arrived safely back on Earth.

APOLLO 15
JULY 26 TO AUGUST 7, 1971

In the fourth manned Moon
landing, the crew observed the
surface, took photographs, and
conducted experiments, in addi-
tion to implementing the first use
of the Lunar Roving Vehicle.

APOLLO 12
NOVEMBER 14 TO 24, 1969

Apollo 12 was a precision
lunar landing mission
intended to conduct sur-
face experiments, as well
as recover the Surveyor III,
which had landed on the
Moon on April 20, 1967.

APOLLO 14
JANUARY 31 TO
FEBRUARY 9, 1971

The third manned Moon
landing, this mission
included exploration,
photography, sample
collection, and even an
astronaut playing golf on
the surface of the Moon.

APOLLO 16
APRIL 16 TO 27, 1972

The second lunar mis-
sion to use the Lunar
Roving Vehicle, this
mission focused on
exploring the surface
of the Moon, as well
as conducing surface
experiments.

APOLLO 17
DECEMBER 7 TO 19, 1972

The last manned lunar
mission and the last
mission in Project Apollo,
this mission included
geological experiments,
as well as surface tests
and exploration.

APOLLO 11: ONE GIANT LEAP FOR MANKIND

The Apollo 11 mission launched from Cape Canaveral, Florida, on July 16, 1969, with a crew of three astronauts: Commander Neil Armstrong, Lunar Module Pilot Edwin "Buzz" Aldrin, and Command Module Pilot Michael Collins.

After a nail-biting landing where the Lunar Module nearly ran out of fuel, Neil Armstrong took mankind's first steps on the Moon on July 20, 1969. Over 530 million people (15% of the world's population at the time) watched the landing on television as Armstrong made the now-famous statement "That's one small step for a man, one giant leap for mankind."

All in all, the crew of Apollo 11 traveled a total of 953,054 miles (1,533,797 km)— the equivalent to driving around Earth 38 times.

THE APOLLO 11 CREW

NEIL ARMSTRONG

ROLE IN APOLLO 11: Commander

COSMIC DATA: Neil Armstrong worked as an engineer, test pilot, astronaut, and eventually administrator for NASA during his lifetime. His famous "one giant leap" speech on the surface of the Moon was broadcast around the world on July 20, 1969. He took many of the photographs on the Apollo 11 mission and was the first man to walk on the Moon.

EDWIN "BUZZ" ALDRIN

ROLE IN APOLLO 11: Lunar Module Pilot

COSMIC DATA: Thanks to his four-day flight on the *Gemini XII* spacecraft, Aldrin was the perfect candidate to pilot the Lunar Module *Eagle*, both during its landing and to connect the Lunar Module back to the Command Module after landing. He was the second man to walk on the Moon.

MICHAEL COLLINS

ROLE IN APOLLO 11: Command Module Pilot

COSMIC DATA: Michael Collins was part of the third group of astronauts named by NASA in 1963. He flew on the Gemini X mission before the Apollo 11 mission, which gave him the experience to be in charge of the Command Module while Neil Armstrong and Edwin "Buzz" Aldrin were on the Moon. Collins is the only member of the Apollo 11 crew who did not walk on the surface of the Moon.

SATURN V

One of the most famous rockets is Saturn V, which NASA used to send astronauts to the Moon during the Apollo program. It was taller than the Statue of Liberty, and it was extremely powerful. Saturn V could launch the weight of about four school buses all the way to the Moon! There were many different Saturn V rockets built over the years. The last one launched in 1973, and it carried the Skylab space station into Earth's orbit. Today, scientists continue to develop more and more powerful rockets all the time.

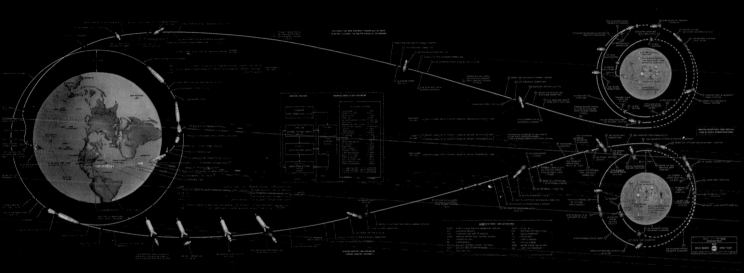

Getting from Earth to the Moon takes a lot of planning—and a lot of math—since one wrong calculation could easily cause an emergency situation. This image shows the path of the Apollo 11 mission in detail.

HISTORIC FLIGHT

In order to get into space, rockets have to generate a lot of power. This is because they have to fight against Earth's gravitational pull. Once in space, the Saturn V rocket made an orbit around Earth, and then used Earth's gravity like a slingshot to launch it toward the Moon. This same method was used to leave the Moon, but instead of having to launch a full rocket, the Lunar Module landed on the surface of the Moon while the Command Module stayed in orbit. Then, the Lunar Module flew back up to join with the Command Module, dropped off the astronauts, and fell back to the surface of the Moon. The Command Module then used the Moon's gravity to return to Earth.

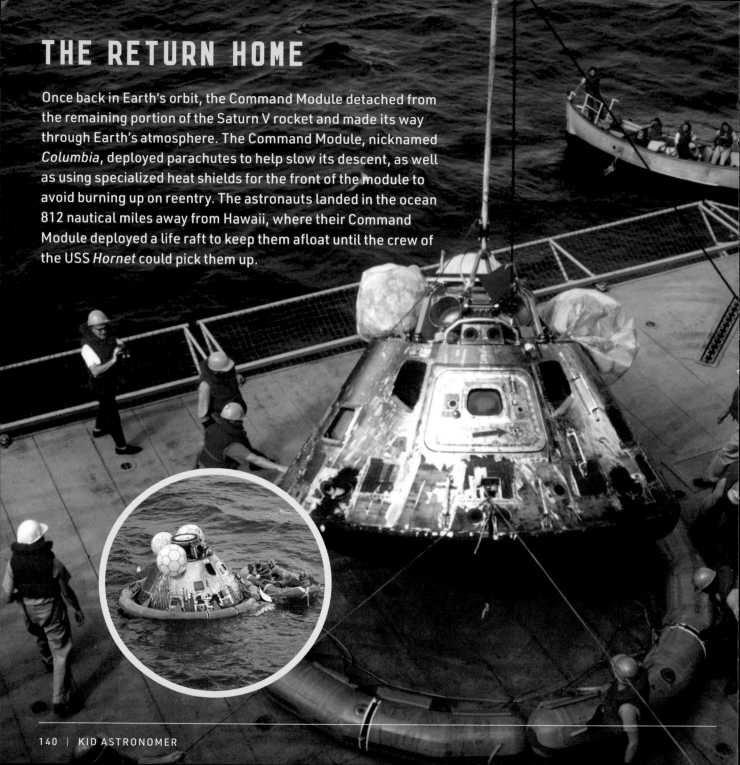

THE RETURN HOME

Once back in Earth's orbit, the Command Module detached from the remaining portion of the Saturn V rocket and made its way through Earth's atmosphere. The Command Module, nicknamed *Columbia*, deployed parachutes to help slow its descent, as well as using specialized heat shields for the front of the module to avoid burning up on reentry. The astronauts landed in the ocean 812 nautical miles away from Hawaii, where their Command Module deployed a life raft to keep them afloat until the crew of the USS *Hornet* could pick them up.

THE LAST MAN ON THE MOON

Thanks to the following six Apollo missions, scientists discovered information about the mineral makeup and atmospheric conditions of the Moon, carried out solar wind experiments, and tested for seismic activity.

The last Apollo mission was the Apollo 17 mission in 1972, during which the crew discovered evidence of 3.6-billion-year-old volcanic ash. This marks the last manned visit to the Moon. However, various robotic missions have been carried out to this day.

Even though the last Apollo program ended, NASA is always looking out into our solar system to discover more. NASA may be sending another manned mission to the Moon in the near future. With plans for a Lunar Orbital Platform-Gateway set to orbit around the Moon and act as a waypoint (a stopping place on a journey) for future missions, NASA is preparing for the next manned space mission—this time to Mars. The Gateway could also function as a live-in research base for astronauts, allowing scientists to further study deep space.

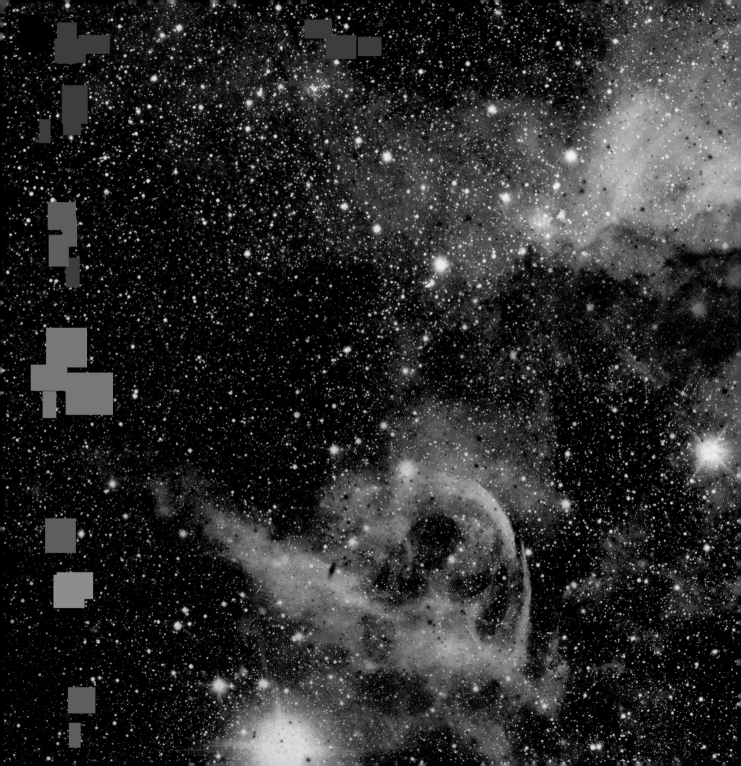

Pages 59, 94, 95, 97, 109 (small photo), 117, 138, 140 (small photo), and 141 courtesy of NASA; page 63 courtesy of Creative Commons/PlanetUser; page 70 courtesy of ESO/L. Calcada and Nick Risinger (skysurvey.org); page 110 courtesy of NASA Ames; pages 111 and 124 courtesy of NASA/JPL-Caltech/MSS; pages 116, 123, 126-127, 131 (Pioneer 1), 139, and 140 courtesy of NASA/JPL-Caltech; pages 113 (small photo) and 120-121 courtesy of NASA/ JPL; page 125 courtesy of NASA/JPL-Caltech/ASU/MSSS

All other images used under official license from Shutterstock.com

ABOUT
APPLESAUCE PRESS

Good ideas ripen with time. From seed to harvest, Applesauce Press crafts books with beautiful designs, creative formats, and kid-friendly information on a variety of fascinating topics. Like our parent company, Cider Mill Press Book Publishers, our press bears fruit twice a year, publishing a new crop of titles each spring and fall.

"Where good books are ready for press"
501 Nelson Place
Nashville, Tennessee 37214

cidermillpress.com